THE
MUSEUMS OF
MEXICO CITY

Susana Martínez-Ostos
and
Clive Alexander Bayne

illustrations by
Susana Martínez-Ostos

Published by
Publicaciones Pirámide, S.A. de C.V.

The Museums of Mexico City is published by
Publicaciones Pirámide, S.A. de C.V.
Lago Silverio 224
Col. Anáhuac
México, D.F. 11320

PIRAMIDE is a trade mark of
Publicaciones Pirámide, S.A. de C.V.

© 1989 Publicaciones Pirámide, S.A. de C.V.

ISBN 968-6070-03-6

Cover illustration by Susana Martínez-Ostos
Cover design by Luz Mari Morales de Rivas

Set in Benguiat and Helvetica
Design and production by FOTOEDISA
Laguna de Mayrán 258, 11320-México, D.F.

Printed and bound in Mexico

Acknowledgments

A great number of people have offered their encouragement, support and suggestions during the writing of this book. In particular, we wish to acknowledge the contributions made by Jorge Martín Cadena; Elizabeth Cuéllar; Raúl Martínez-Ostos I; Adela Pisarro Suárez de Prieto; Luis Javier Solana and Paco Ignacio Taibo I. Also we would like to thank all those museum directors who took time to answer the many questions about their museums and who were always kind enough to give us the necessary support to do our research. To all of them we owe a great debt of gratitude.

THE AUTHORS
Mexico City 1989

Contents

Introduction   7

Some notes for visitors   9

Museums by type   11

A - Z of Entries   15

Alphabetical list of museums   139

Maps   141

Introduction

The story of Mexico's growth and development over nearly seven hundred years is an astonishing epic. Long and complicated, but never dull, it threads through centuries of myth, history and outstanding cultural achievement with the country's legendary color and magic never far beneath the surface. The legacy is one that is admired throughout the world.

A grand part of this country's heritage is displayed in the many fine museums open to the public in Mexico City. This book has been written and illustrated to encourage residents and visitors alike to explore these fascinating collections. Not only does the text describe and evaluate sixty-four museums, but it also provides the necessary background information in the form of historical or cultural perspectives for them to be appreciated by the non-specialist visitor.

Compiling the material for this book rewarded us with a greater understanding of the documentary drama of Mexico's rich history and accomplishments. It is now published as a guide for all who wish to acquire a more intimate knowledge of the exceptional country in which they are living or visiting.

THE AUTHORS
Mexico City 1989

Some notes for visitors

Opening times: These are given for each museum but they are subject to change without notice. As a general rule, most museums are open on Sundays and are closed on Mondays. However, most museums will be closed on the national Mexican holidays, a list of which is given below.

National Holidays: For the Republic of Mexico the annual national holidays are:

January	1	New Year's Day
February	5	Constitution Day
February	24	National Flag Day
March	21	Birthday of Benito Juárez
Variable		Holy Thursday
Variable		Good Friday
May	1	Labor Day
May	5	Battle of Puebla
September	16	Independence Day
October	12	Christopher Columbus Day
November	1	Presidential Report
		All Saints Day
November	2	All Souls Day
November	20	Revolution Day
December	25	Christmas Day

Entry charges: Many museums in Mexico City make no entry charge and even those that do allow free entry on Sundays (except private museums). Where entry charges exist, they tend to be minimal and can vary from as little as the equivalent of twenty U.S. cents to one U.S. dollar.

Museum information: Almost without exception, the information about exhibits in the museums covered in this book is only available in Spanish. It is to be hoped that this policy will change in the future as Mexico City boasts a number of internationally renowned museums which would benefit from having more information available in other major languages.

Museums by Type

Anthropology and Archeological Museums

Anahuacalli Museum
Anthropology. National Museum of
Anthropology. University Museum of
Cuicuilco. Archeological Museum of
Templo Mayor Museum
Xochimilco. Archeological Museum of

Art Museums (Paintings)

Alameda Museum (Diego Rivera Mural)
Art. National Museum of
Bellas Artes. Museum of the Palace of
Carrillo Gil Museum of Art
Chopo University Museum
Contemporary Art Cultural Center
Franz Mayer Museum
La Profesa. Art Gallery of the Church of
Modern Art Museum
Rufino Tamayo Museum
San Carlos Museum
San Diego. Viceroy Art Gallery of
Watercolors. Museum of

Art Museums (Plastic and Applied)

Architecture. National Museum of
Caricature. Museum of
Cathedral Museum
Contemporary Art Cultural Center
Franz Mayer Museum
Geles Cabrera Museum of Sculpture
Printing. National Museum of

Biographic Museums

Alfonso Reyes. House and Museum of
Benito Juárez. Museum in Honor of
Carranza. House and Museum of
Diego Rivera Studio Museum
Frida Kahlo Museum
Leon Trotsky Museum
Siqueiros Public Art Gallery
Sor Juana Inés de la Cruz. Cloister of
Wax Museum. Mexico City

Cultural History Museums

Charrería. Museum of
Cultures. National Museum of
Mexican Clothing. Luis Márquez Romay Museum of
Mexican Medicine. Museum of the History of
Musical Instruments. National Museum of
Popular Arts and Industries. National Museum of
Popular Cultures. National Museum of

General Museums

El Carmen. Museum of
Guadalupe Basilica Museum
Mexico City Museum
Risco House Museum
Santo Domingo Cultural Center (Juan Cordero Room)

History Museums

History. National Museum of
History. Gallery of the National Museum of (Snail Museum)
Interventions. National Museum of
Mexico City Museum
Parliamentary Enclosure
Revolution. National Museum of the

Literary Museums

Alfonso Reyes. House and Museum of
Remembrance. Museum of

Science and Technology Museums

Geology Museum
Marine Grotto
Natural History Museum
Technology. Museum of
See University City Complex. Museums in the

Miscellaneous Specialist Museums

Postal Museum

Alameda Museum
(Diego Rivera Mural)
Museo de la Alameda

Plaza de la Solidaridad, Col. Centro

Open: Tuesday to Sunday 10.00 am to 6.00 pm

Map 1

Diego Rivera's famous mural, *Sueño de una Tarde Dominical en la Alameda Central* (A Sunday Afternoon Dream in the Alameda) was begun in 1947 and finished in June 1948. It was commissioned for the dining room of the Hotel del Prado in Avenida Juárez opposite the Alameda Park. The hotel was damaged so seriously in the 1985 earthquakes that it had to be demolished. Fortunately, the mural masterpiece survived the earthquakes but a new home had to be found for it. In the end, a brand new salon was constructed to house it in the new Plaza de Solidaridad almost opposite the site of the old hotel.

It is impossible to overestimate the engineering challenge that the removal of this enormous mural to its new home presented to the authorities. In fact, apart from the picture itself, one of the most interesting aspects of this museum is a chronological collection of color photographs and drawings which have been preserved to document this extraordinary undertaking. It was a notable example of how an important piece of art can be salvaged against incredible odds if the desire and motivation are there.

This purpose-built salon contains only this one item. It was constructed after painstaking research into possible locations and only after the technical problems relative to the subsoil in this earthquake-prone area of town had been thoroughly investigated.

The mural is now displayed on the far wall of a vast hall. The space is modern, well designed and well lit. At just the right distance from the mural are two long glass-covered cases which contain drawn-to-scale silhouettes of all the characters in the mural with reference numbers for their names.

This superlative painting is not to be missed. It catches all the movement and liveliness of Mexico City. In the far right hand corner of the mural a Mexican family sit at a little wooden table, absorbed in their meal, almost under the hooves of a soldier's monstruous rearing horse. In the same way today in the Alameda, tables are set up on crowded sidewalks, buses and cars taking the place of horses. The whole panorama presents a history lesson and an insight into Mexican customs at one sweeping glance. Rivera himself appears in the center of the mural painted as a grotesque child, hand-in-hand with his bride. The bride is a grinning death's head beneath the flowers and veil - a tribute to the great illustrator, Posada, a friend and contemporary of Rivera's. Behind them stands Frida Kahlo, the painter's third wife in real life.

Sueño de un Tarde Dominical en la Alameda Central has always been in the news ever since it was first unveiled. Originally, Rivera had painted Ignacio Ramírez, the necromancer, holding a phrase which said, *Dios no existe* (God does not exist). This caused such a furor that Rivera was finally forced to replace it with a less controversial phrase.

House and Museum of Alfonso Reyes
Capilla Alfonsina

Benjamin Hill 122, Col. Hipódromo Condesa

Open: Monday to Saturday 11.00 am to 3.00 pm

Alfonso Reyes was born in Monterrey in 1889 and died in Mexico City in 1959. He was indisputedly one of Mexico's great literati. His published literary output embraced short stories, poetry, essays and criticism. At the age of twenty-six he published his *Visión de Anáhuac*, a book about what Hernán Cortés found on arriving in Tenochtitlán. It is one of his many classics and is required reading in no less a place than the Sorbonne in Paris. His dramatic poem, *Ifegenia Cruel*, published in 1926, assured him a place as one of Latin America's foremost poets.

Apart from his writing, Reyes, a lawyer by training, was a successful career diplomat. He served his country in key embassy posts in France and Spain and was appointed Mexican ambassador to Brazil and, twice, to Argentina. On his return to Mexico City in 1939, he helped the many Spanish exiles of that time and, in 1940, was instrumental in setting up the Colegio de México. This is one of the country's most reputable educational establishments and Reyes was appointed its first president. In 1946 he headed the Mexican delegation to the first international UNESCO assembly in Paris.

His house and extensive library were converted into a museum in 1981 under the direction of Raquel Tiból. Today it is administered by Alfono Reyes' grand daughter, Alicia Reyes. In Spanish it has always been known as the *Capilla Alfonsina* (chapel or sanctuary). The reason being that his friend, Enrique Díez-Canedo, always referred to Alfonso Reyes' house as 'a sanctuary of knowledge'. It was an impressive, and lasting compliment.

On view are a number of rooms in which are displayed photographs, an impressive collection of letters, documents, diplomas and paintings as well as the simple household objects and furniture that made up the Reyes home. The exhibition follows a parallel text approach as if one were reading two pages of a book. On one page is the story of the writer himself, while on the other is the story of what was happening in Mexico at the same time. It is an inspired idea that works well.

The library takes up more space than the rest of the house put together. It is now used as a center for literary studies for university students and researchers.

Alfonso Reyes is held in very high regard both in his own country and abroad. Ever since 1909 when he founded the *Ateneo de la Juventud* literary group (Vasconcelos, Antonio Caso and Martín Luis Gúzman were among its members), Alfonso Reyes was always in the vanguard of Mexican literature. He combined modesty and kindness with considerable charisma. In 1944 he remarked that, "each individual looks at the world through a special window - mine is literature". The father-in-law of one of the present authors knew him well. "He was a great man in all senses, totally honest in his life and in his work". There can be few more appealing epigraphs than that.

Anahuacalli Museum
Museo Anahuacalli

Calle del Museo 150, Col. San Pablo Tepetlapa   Map 6

Open: Tuesday to Sunday 10.00 am to 6.00 pm

Diego Rivera, apart from being one of Mexico's finest painters and muralists, was also a major collector of archeological treasures. This museum was designed and built by him to house some two thousand of his seven-thousand-piece pre-Hispanic archeological collection. Shortly before his death in 1957, the artist donated both the museum and its priceless contents to the Mexican nation.

"I return to the people the artistic inheritance I was able to redeeem from their ancestors," he wrote. This text is inscribed on the plate of volcanic rock marking the entrance to this important museum which, to this day, is still under the direction of Dolores Olmeda, Rivera's model, patron and life-long friend. The word *anahuacalli* means house of the Aná-huac (the Indian name for the Valley of Mexico meaning 'near the water').

The building is massive, made almost entirely of dark-gray volcanic rock hewn from the lava bed on which it is built. The design is eminently original, and resembles an ancient pyramid which, according to the designer himself, "is a combination of Aztec, Mayan and Rivera styles". Inaugurated as a museum in 1964, it contains twenty-three exhibition rooms which are organized chronologically.

Somewhat dusty and neglected, the Anahuacalli still displays some of the finest examples of Mexico's cultural past in an extraordinary and unforgettable setting of visionary architecture. Exhibited here are tall stone sculptures, baked-clay figurines and pottery from the Aztec and Teotihuacan cultures. An important collection of Huastecan sculptures dating back to the fourth and fifth centuries B.C. are also among the treasures of the Anahuacalli.

On the second floor, Rivera built a studio which he never lived to use. This contains his last unfinished paintings, his first drawing at the age of three, and a fascinating miscellany of Aztec mural poems, photographs, indigenous objects and some charcoal sketches on a grand scale.

The Anahuacalli Museum

From the museum's flat roof, one can view the chain of extinct volcanoes that surround the city. Unfortunately, the urban sprawl has long since overrun the wild, rocky landscape that Rivera chose as the ideal site for his museum. Nevertheless, one can still feel the overwhelming impact of his achievement and vision in creating the Anahuacalli. The building and its contents are a consecration to Mexico's ancient civilizations - civilizations which, on this spot, seem as all pervasive as ever.

National Museum of Anthropology
Museo Nacional de Antropología

Paseo de la Reforma y Gandhi
Col. Bosque de Chapultepec   Map 3

Open: Tuesday to Saturday 9.00 am to 7.00 pm
        Sundays and holidays 10.00 am to 6.00 pm

When the National Museum of Anthropology was inaugurated in September 1964, Mexico succeeded in accomplishing something very notable from the standpoint of museum science. From whatever angle one begins to appreciate this visionary undertaking - the cultural material it exhibits, its manner of presentation or the museum building itself - one is left almost breathless in admiration. In a comparatively short period of time, this museum has established itself as one of the finest and most functional in existence anywhere in the world. If a visitor to Mexico City were to do no more than just visit this museum, the visit would not have been in vain.

Architecture: Designed by Pedro Ramírez Vázquez, the National Museum of Anthropology cleverly accomodates certain pre-Hispanic architectural values which still have some relevance today. The huge open spaces and the use of materials which are left to show off their natural colors and textures combine with forms that resonate with ancient Mesoamerican cultures. The museum's patio, for example, respects the proportions and aesthetics of Mayan architecture, while its facades recall the simplicity and severity of Teotihuacan.

The design is precise and clean. The vast central patio acts both as a focal point and a space distributor. Each of the museum's twenty-three principal galleries on two levels are accessible either individually or as part of a complete circuit. Even with the complete circuit approach, visitors are returned to the patio after every two exhibit areas. Congestion is thereby avoided and compulsory pauses, or short periods of relaxation, are subtly interposed. The fountain in the patio, under an umbrella-like construction supported by a central single column, is noteworthy. This overhead cover, at once independent and integrated into the whole patio design, functions both as a protection against the elements and as a harmonious link between sculpture and architecture. Time and again the museum's construction draws one back to the central patio area which succeeds in creating the same sensation of spatial grandeur as that found in pre-Hispanic structures.

The material on display: Mexico did not start out on the path of scientifically studying its past until the second half of the nineteenth century. Serious archeological and anthropological studies can be dated from 1865; but since the Mexican revolution in 1910, studies in all fields of anthropology have increased sharply. The result of this work, apart from an enormous depository of knowledge, has been the acquisition of a countless number of objects and artifacts which now form the basis of the museum's collections. Exhibits trace the history of Mexico from the country's origins to those great architectural structures that marked the zenith of pre-Hispanic Mesoamerican civilizations, and beyond to an ethnographic study of present-day Mexico.

Exhibits on the main floor (halls 1 to 12) are organized historically within the context of particular geographic and cultural areas. In addition, there are three halls covering an introduction to the science of anthropology and Mesoamerican culture, and a history of the Valley of Mexico. Remaining halls on the ground floor cover the flowering the Teotihuacan, Toltec and Aztec civilizations; the cultures of the Oaxacan, Gulf Coast and Mayan areas as well as the cultures on the fringes of Mesoamerica in the Northern and Western regions of Mexico.

The upper floor of the museum (halls 1 to 11) is devoted

Warrior's head from Palenque
National Museum of Anthropology

to present-day ethnographic exhibits of the cultures displayed directly below. These exhibits, which include life-size reconstructions of domestic dwellings, clothes and everyday objects, are a vivid reminder of the fact that some eight percent of the Mexican population is still made up of indigenous communities that still retain their own traditions, customs and languages.

Presentation of the exhibits: In the initial planning stage, the National Museum of Anthropology sought to achieve three objectives: to preserve extensive archeological and ethnological collections, to support continued investigation and study of these valuable materials and to disseminate knowledge to both Mexicans and visitors from abroad. Several of the collections contain archeological pieces that are considered outstanding examples of universal art. However, the museum's organizers have avoided falling into the trap of emphasizing the artistic value of each great work at the expense of setting them in their chronological sequence. The result is a museum that strikes the correct balance between art and science.

The overall presentation of exhibits is uncluttered and well spaced. Natural and artificial light combine to relieve the feeling of claustrophobia often experienced in many other large-scale museums. Throughout the halls, original archeological material is cleverly interspersed with scale-sized reconstructions, models of ancient sites, dioramas and panoramas.

However, the first-time visitor should be warned: good though the presentation is, the sheer wealth of material can be overwhelming. Explanatory notes are only in Spanish (inexplicable for such an international museum), and more than one visit is necessary before a sense of the whole can be grasped.

In the entrance hall there is an orientation room which offers a twenty-minute audiovisual presentation on Mesoamerican culture (only in Spanish), an auditorium, a temporary exhibition room and the library. The famous Florentine codices are in the latter. In addition, there is a restaurant and a very well-stocked book and gift shop.

National Museum of Architecture
Museo Nacional de Arquitectura

Palace of Fine Arts (Bellas Artes)
Av. Juárez and Lázaro Cárdenas, Col. Centro   Map1

Open: Tuesday to Sunday 10.30 am to 6.30 pm

This small museum opened in 1984 and is housed on the fourth floor of the Bellas Artes Palace (see entry). There is no permanent exhibition, but the space is regularly given over to temporary displays of the works of Mexico's more famous architects. The contents are usually drawings, plans and photographs covering a certain architectural period, a specific style or a particular project. The details of each exhibit are advertised in the main foyer of Bellas Artes.

National Museum of Art
Museo Nacional de Arte

Tacuba 8, Col. Centro   Map 1

Open: Wednesday to Sunday 10.00 am to 6.00 pm

In 1904, Porfirio Díaz ordered the construction of this neo-renaissance government palace which was built by the Italian architect, Silvio Contri. The Palace of Communications and Public Works was completed in 1911. When this government department outgrew the palace, it served as a repository for the General National Archives before becoming the National Museum of Art in 1982.

The three-storey building with its gray-stone facade is enhanced by considerable ironwork and wooden window frames. The equestrian statue of Charles IV, a masterpiece by Spanish sculptor and architect Manuel Tolsá, graces the small plaza in front of the building and adds to the palatial tone. This is a cold, majestic, gray building of the old-fashioned museum type with which visitors from Europe will be only too familiar.

The exhibition floors are reached by climbing Contri's spectacular marble and iron staircase. Here is an outstandingly rich collection of paintings (some seven hundred works in all) covering the development of Mexican art from the colonial period to the mid-twentieth century.

The development of Mexican painting: A visit to this fine museum is best understood within an historical framework of the development of painting in Mexico. In 1523 Friar Pedro de Gante founded a school for native Mexicans in which they were taught Western techniques of music, sculpture and painting. A body of work was gradually formed where religious and everyday scenes could be used for the cultural education of the masses. In the first few galleries the vast majority of paintings are steeped in religious symbolism.

In 1785 the San Carlos Academy of Art was founded by the Viceroy Conde de Gálvez. The academy taught the basic principles of perspective, drawing and painting. In Europe, romanticism was beginning to develop, not so much as a style but as a form of sensibility. Mexico provided a wealth of new material for European Romantic painters and they were welcomed in the country with open arms. The English landscape painter, Daniel Thomas Egerton, is considered the greatest of these foreign painters who came to Mexico at that time. Another was the German Juan Moritz Rugendas.

In 1846 four talented and enthusiastic young artists arrived in Mexico: Pelegrín Clavé and Manuel Vilar from Spain and Eugenio Landesio and Javier Cavallari from Italy. These four basically monopolized the Academy of San Carlos: Clavé and Vilar took over the painting and sculpture departments of the academy and Landesio and Cavallari directed work in landscape painting and architecture. The influence of these four dedicated artists and teachers cannot be underestimated. On their arrival, the academy was in poor shape but over the ensuing years they managed to breath new life into it. Their group of enthusiastic disciples grew, and in their turn, the pupils developed and branched into new subject matter. Clavé was much in demand for portraits and also developed a taste for religious and biblical themes, considering them to be major art since, "they fulfill a moral commitment as well as an artistic one." Much of his work from this period is on view in the gallery.

Landesio's inspired landscapes hang side by side with those of his famous pupil, José María Velasco. Their rigorous training in perspective and drawing, color, texture and the effect of light result in these breathtaking and glorious paintings.

Many of the students in the academy at that time were scholarship pupils who had come from the provinces. They had little time to study at the academy and soon returned to their native towns and villages. Together they helped form what has come to be known as the mainly anonymous school of Mexican primitive art.

Mexican primitive art: This school is richly represented in the National Museum of Art and merits a more detailed explanation. Throughout the Mexican provinces there appeared in the nineteenth century, almost spontaneously, a wave of painting known as *pintura popular*. This school produced a substantial mass of work, diverse in both quality and theme. Many artists who formed part of this movement worked in provincial towns which were beyond the reach of the theory and teaching of the Academy of San Carlos in Mexico City. Some of them had perhaps studied there briefly before returning to their homes. Portrait painting, previously a rich field for academy artists in the eighteenth century, became equally remunerative for these provincial painters a century later. It now became the turn of the small-town leaders and the bourgeois big-wigs to have their portraits painted both in life and in death. This curious post mortem genre of primitive portraiture was highly lucrative for many of these painters. José María Estrada and Hermenegildo Bustos stand out especially in this genre. Another theme faithfully covered by primitive painters was that of folk and regional customs, both in the small towns and in the countryside. Pedro Patiño Ixtolinque and Ernesto Icaza are two other painters from this school well represented here. Today, these primitive Mexican paintings are our only opportunity to glimpse a lost world.

Later developments: In 1867 Clavé was appointed director of the Academy of San Carlos much to the chagrin of the Puebla artist, Juan Cordero. The latter had been away studying in Rome and became incensed on returning to find the academy wholly in the grips of foreigners. Unfortunately for Cordero, critics still consider Clavé to have been by far the more accomplished painter. A considerable quantity of the works of both these artists are on display so visitors can draw their own conclusions as to their respective merits.

Towards the end of the nineteenth century and into the twentieth, the academy again fell into decline. By that time 'revolutionary art' was beginning to flourish elsewhere but in far less academic circles. There is a good collection of Posada drawings and engravings in the museum from this period. The last gallery in the museum which might be labeled 'the academy in decline' should not, however, be entirely written off. It contains some curious and often enchanting paintings in a style which everyday become more fashionable in international art circles. Oscaranza's *La Flor Machita* is a fine example of one such painting.

When there were no museums in Mexico, paintings were hidden away in private collections, crowded in darkened churches or just lay forgotten in cupboards and attics. It was only at the beginning of the present century that the idea caught on of collecting them together. Fortunately, we can now see this fabulous collection of paintings displayed according to themes and dated. This museum has excelled in bringing together the best of four centuries of Mexican art.

Museum of the Palace of Bellas Artes
Museo del Palacio de Bellas Artes

Av. Juárez and Lázaro Cárdenas
Col. Centro   Map 1

Open: Tuesday to Sunday 10.30 am to 6.30 pm

The Bellas Artes Palace is undoubtedly one of Mexico City's bolder landmarks. Its architectural style defies classification: *art nouveau* might be the nearest for the exterior, with *art deco* being more than adequate for the interior. In fact it took over thirty years (1904 - 1934) to be completed, and it became the brainchild of two master architects and scores of artists, mostly foreign, before it was inaugurated. Experts like to refer to its character as being more *sui generis* than anything else, while for those of us who eschew Latin tags, it often reminds us of a rather attractive wedding cake.

The Italian architect Adamo Boari initiated the project, which was originally designed to be a national theatre, in the closing years of the Porfiriato. The Mexican Revolution (1910-1920) caused both the work to stop and Boari to flee the country. He left with most of the exterior finished and, when the country returned to more tranquil times, Mexican architect Federico Mariscal completed the work. By then the original commission had been changed to palace of fine arts instead of theatre. Mariscal's *art deco* interior conception was certainly in tune with what was happening in Europe and the States at that time. The term *art deco* had only been coined a few years earlier (it derives from the *Exposition des Arts Décoratifs et Industriels Modernes* held in Paris in 1925), so the palace which Mexico eventually inherited certainly compensated for its long gestation by making a fashion-conscious début.

The palace boasts nine exhibition areas spread over four floors and a huge theatre. The display rooms tend to be rather confusingly distributed, and one can find oneself chasing upstairs, downstairs and round the corner in order to see everything. However, the noise of squeaking parquet floors (that most authentic of museum sounds) can be enjoyed in most of them. There is invariably an artistic bustle about the place: people coming and going from meetings, buying theatre tickets, wandering in and out of the temporary exhibitions, or even a visiting orchestra admiring the view. The visitor can only be assured of the permanence of the building and the murals. These latter decorate the walls giving onto the central covered space on all of the first three floors. A large sign in the entrance hall announces that works by José Clemente Orozco, Diego Rivera, David Alfaro Siqueiros, Roberto Montenegro, Rufino Tamayo and Jorge González Camarena are here to be admired.

It is difficult not to be totally absorbed by the streamlined *art deco* interior with its geometric and stylized ornamentation as one climbs up towards the palace's crowning glory - the dome. On every floor there are exhibition rooms with often misleading names. The Sala Diego Rivera, for instance, is not full of his paintings but just another part of the exhibition room plan. The murals are best appreciated from the opposite sides of the gallery. They all burst with idealistic vigor and, together, form a fine introduction to Mexican revolutionary art. Lozano's *La Piedad en el Desierto* (The Virgin Mary and the Suffering Christ in the Desert), painted in 1941, comes as quite a shock on the third floor after all those revolutionary fists below. This was painted in jail - Lozano had been convicted of stealing three paintings while Director of the National Academy of Plastic Arts and sentenced to prison. Twenty-five years later the said paintings mysteriously reappeared which would appear to exonerate Lozano.

On the fourth floor of the palace is the National Museum of Architecture (see entry). On the ground floor, a well-stocked bookshop and a small cafeteria make pleasant breaks after indulging in one of the city's most exuberant museum experiences.

Museum of Caricature
Museo de la Caricatura

Antiguo Colegio de Cristo
Donceles 99, Col. Centro   Map 6

Open: Tuesday to Sunday 10.30 am to 6.00 pm

This ancient college building, once El Colegio de Cristo, dates from the 1770s and is considered to be one of the finest examples of Mexican colonial architecture of its time. Every year it draws thousands of visitors who are exploring the historic downtown area of the city. It now houses a museum dedicated to the works of Mexico's caricaturists, past and present.

The exhibitions are temporary and tend to focus on the work of one particular cartoonist. The display areas occupy a number of small narrow rooms around the central courtyard of the ancient college. Overflow space is sometimes used on the opposite side of the patio. Perhaps because cartoonists feel a latent unease at having their work mounted for serious inspection, there seems to be a palpable lack of enthusiasm here. It is very much a take-it-or-leave-it museum which does little to trumpet its existence.

Inside the doorway —preserved as if in a time capsule— is the building's directory still with the nameplates hand-painted on tile. Even the art of caricature is hard pressed to deliver that sort of immortality!

Museum and House of Carranza
Museo de los Constituyentes
o Venustiano Carranza

Río Lerma 35, Col. Cuauhtémoc   Map 5

Open: Tuesday to Saturday 9.00 am to 6.00 pm
    Sundays 11.00 am to 3.00 pm

The Mexican Revolution of 1910 ousted Porfirio Díaz from power and ushered in a period of intense civil war which lasted until 1920. The first revolutionary president, Francisco Madero (1911-1913) had attempted a well-meaning but ineffectual experiment with democracy. He failed because he had urged caution and moderation on the burning social issues of the day. His successor, Victoriano Huerta (1913-1914), was no more successful. His style was dictatorial and while he was not unwilling to give social reformers the chance to institute change, many Mexicans could not bring themselves to accomodate another brutal dictatorship which exalted order at the expense of liberty.

It was Venustiano Carranza, as Governor of Coahuila State, who was among the first not to recognize the new Huerta regime. In March 1913 Carranza and others drew up the *Plan de Guadalupe* which nominated Carranza as the First Chief of the Constitutionalist army. Huerta thus found himself fighting on two fronts: the Constitutionalists in the North and Emiliano Zapata in the South. Against overwhelming military odds, Huerta resigned in July 1914.

The years following Huerta's departure are the most chaotic in Mexican revolutionary history as quarrels between erstwhile allies intensified. The early months of 1915 saw the Mexican Revolution degenerating into unmitigated anarchy. Civil wars ravaged many states. In Washington, President Wilson decided to throw official support behind Carranza's Constitutionalists. In November 1916, Carranza convened a conference in the city of Querétaro in an attempt to legitimize the Revolution. In an attempt to control the proceedings, Carranza submitted to the Querétaro conference the draft of a new Constitution of which he himself approved. After fierce debate, a new Constitution emerged from Querétaro which bore scant resemblance to the draft Carranza had originally proposed. However, he agreed to abide by it. Carranza won the special presidential elections that were held in March 1917 and took the oath of office on May 1. After years of civil strife, the country's economy was in a state of acute distress, and the country was far from pacified.

Carranza quickly let it be known that while he had accepted the 1917 Constitution, he had little idea of enforc-° ing it. In essence, he had confused a change in government with a change in society. He believed the Revolution to be over. In fact, it had scarcely begun.

There can be little doubt that Carranza's presidency was complicated by World War I. However, that was no reason for Carranza's refusal to accelerate the pace of the Mexican Revolution, with the redistribution of land as one of its central tenets. Of all the disillusioned revolutionary groups in Mexico, the Zapatistas remained the most ardent. Carranza eventually concocted a plan to assasinate Zapata and in April 1919 he had ridded himself of his most implacable adversary. It proved to be a prophetic move for, in May 1920, Carranza was forced to flee from Mexico City in the face of mounting opposition from the North. On his way into exile Carranza himself was assasinated by one of his own guards whose loyalty had switched to Alvaro Obregon, the next President of Mexico.

The Carranza regime has perhaps not yet received the careful historical evaluation that it deserves. Despite revolutionary rhetoric, Carranza moved slowly on the issue of social reform. His association with the 1917 Constitution is enough to guarantee him a central place in Mexico's revolutionary history.

The house in which this museum is located was his home for the last few years of his life. It is in the French style of the late Porfiriata and was built in 1908. In 1981 it was converted into a museum having previously been used as an embassy building.

The ground floor is devoted exclusively to the historical documents related to the *Plan de Guadalupe* and the Querétaro Congress which gave birth to the famous 1917 Constitution. On the first floor are the Carranza family bedrooms and his private office. Also on display are the clothes he was wearing on the day he was killed. There is an auditorium and library in the basement of the house where a copy of the original 1917 Constitution can be seen.

Carrillo Gil Museum of Art
Museo de Arte Carrillo Gil

Av. Revolución 1608, Col. San Angel   Map 2

Open: Tuesday to Sunday 9.00 am to 6.00 pm

The building housing this important collection of paintings could easily be mistaken for an office block. There are signs to follow and it is in fact within easy walking distance of the Diego Rivera Studio Museum (see entry). It is the sort of museum that deserves more visitors than it gets.

The building itself was not orginally designed to be a museum. It was bought by the Mexican government from the Carrillo Gil family to house their important private collection which they donated to the country. It opened in 1974 and contains four floors of permanent exhibitions and a gallery for temporary or specialized shows.

The gallery includes a major collection of works by José Clemente Orozco, Diego Rivera, David Alfaro Siqueiros, Wolgang Paalen and Gunter Gerzo. These are indisputably the great men of the last five decades of Mexican art. Orozco, Rivera and Siqueiros were the pillars of the Mexican school which attempted to create monumental art for political education of the people. They invented new techniques, new forms of composition and even new materials. The Carrillo Gil houses the most important collection of Orozco's drawings in Mexico City (most of his work is in his native Guadalajara).

All of these paintings in the Carrillo Gil are magnificent. Orozco's *Paisaje de Picos*, *La Cama Azul*, *La Desesperada* and *El Abrazo* are among the best. Orozco himself commented, "I like the blacks and earth colors excluded from the impressionists' palette." Many of the oils and watercolors exhibited here confirm that predilection: *Colinas Mexicanas*, *El Maguey* and *Mujer* are fine examples. They also illustrate another of his preoccupations: "I undertook to explore the poorest areas of Mexico City."

In hall two, Rivera's *Retrato de Angelina*, *Retrato de un poeta* and his *Angelina y el Niño Diego* are stunning examples of the early Cubist movement (the gallery does not go beyond that period in its permanent collection). Set apart from this school of revolutionary nationalism, but parallel in time, came Carlos Merida, Juan Soriano and Rufino Tamayo. These artists followed routes different from the official school and were joined in the 1940s by Wolgang Paalen and Gunter Gerzo, many of whose works can be enjoyed in halls three and four of this musuem.

The galleries here are spacious and connected via gently inclining ramps. The pictures are well spaced and well lit against white walls. Another important attraction of the Carrillo Gil for Mexico City residents is the full program of well-staged temporary exhibitions and shows which the museum holds throughout the year. The museum also has an excellent bookshop.

Cathedral Museum
Museo del Catedral

Metropolitan Cathedral
Plaza de la Constitución, Col. Centro   Map 1

Open: Tuesday to Sunday 10.00 am to 6.00 pm

The history of Mexico's Cathedral is as complicated as that of the Great Aztec Temple nearby. Both evolved over several centuries and reflected the changing nature of the societies of which they were both the highest expression. This small museum does an invaluable service in charting the progress and construction of both Mexico City's cathedrals - the earlier one begun in 1524 and the present one which was started in 1567 but not finished until 1781.

In the first room are some useful models which locate the present cathedral site in relation to the ancient Aztec ceremonial compound. The overlayering of the Aztec and Spanish cultures is never better illustrated than by the carved stone and other pieces on display which were discovered during various restoration works on the cathedral, some as late as 1976.

In six other rooms, the museum tells the chronological story of the development of both the cathedral's exterior and interior over a period of some four hundred years. The displays mix architectural drawings, mounted color photographs with paintings and other ecclesiastical objects taken from the cathedral's treasure.

The mounting of the photographs and drawings is clear and clean. Several of the rooms have been built out from the exposed walls of the cathedral itself, which inspires an imaginative sense of unity between the site and the museum's contents.

This makes an impressive end to a tour of the Cathedral and Sagrario, and essential for anyone who is interested in studying the varied ways in which these churches have absorbed various architectural styles and the work of hundreds of architects and artists over the centuries.

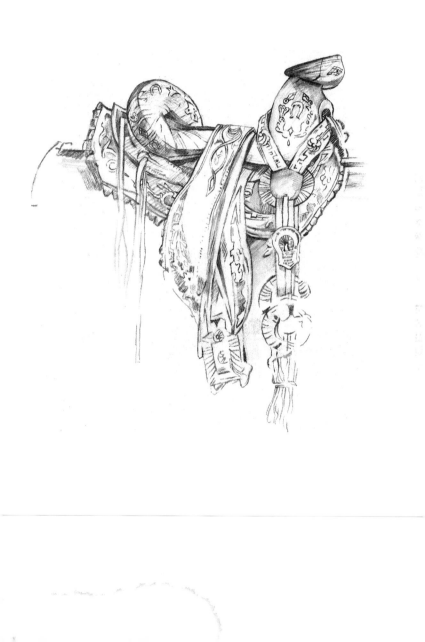

Charro saddle
Museum of Charrería

Museum of Charrería
Museo de la Charrería

Ex-Convento de Montserrat
Isabel la Católica 108, Col. Centro   Map 1

Open: Monday to Friday 9.00 am to 6.00 pm
Saturday 9.00 am to 1.00 pm

Mexicans are ingenious at designing present-day uses for old ex-monasteries or convents. To house a museum dedicated to *charrería* (the word defies translation but 'Mexican horsemanship'gives the idea) in an old Benedictine monastery dating from 1587 has to win some sort of prize for imagination. Since 1973 it has also been the headquarters of the Federación Nacional de Charros which now administers the national sport of *charrería* at all levels, and also runs this museum. Cowboy culture and rodeos are not the sole prerogative of the United States - similar traditions are alive and kicking in Mexico.

After the conquest, indigenous Mexicans were not permitted to ride horses. The Spaniards outlawed not only this but a string of other activities which included the use of fireworks and the playing of musical instruments in church (except the organ). However, in the latter half of the sixteenth century the ban was lifted and the Mexican *charro* developed his own style of riding and his own design of saddles, spurs, lariats and halters as well as a very distinctive dress. While the cultural influences were originally heavily Spanish (the word *charro* itself hails from Salamanca where it originally meant 'boy' or 'lad'), the development of the whole genre is endemic to the Americas. Based on genealogy and historical precedent, the Mexican *charro* is, in fact, father to the North American cowboy.

Perhaps, on second thoughts, the exhibition site is not so well chosen: it is dark and smells of leather, which is understandable, and mould, which is unfortunate. The walls are damp, and in some places, visibly peeling. The vast collection of saddles and and other *charro* gear are rather unimaginatively displayed in serried rows, and frankly, could do with a thorough clean. Perhaps the macho image of the typical *charro* does not countenance the use of a simple cloth and a bottle of Silvo! There are glass cases of *charro* hats, and mannequins dressed in charro costumes including the famous *traje de gala* (popularized by the Emperor Maximilian and used only for exhibitions). Again, the collections are dusty, and they would surely cause many of the famous and sartorially elegant *charros* of yesteryear to at least twitch in their graves. Many of the museum's objects are valuable. They include trophies, a variety of saddle embroidery (red and black being the predominant colors because they were linked to symbols of royalty), sabres, guns, pistol holders, riding crops and even the saddles belonging to Francisco Villa and Maximilian (a great *charro* enthusiast), and a *charro* hat that once graced the head of Porfirio Díaz.

This is a museum more for the dedicated aficionado. *Charros* no longer exist in the countryside (the demise of the hacienda system was theirs as well) and nowadays, paradoxically, they are only to be found in the cities for sporting or tournament purposes. Nevertheless, the *charro* tradition is a colorful and romantic one which this museum succeeds in keeping alive.

The Chopo University Museum
Museo Universitario del Chopo

Enrique González Martínez 10
Col. Santa María la Ribera   Map 5

Open: Wednesday to Sunday 10.00 am to 2.00 pm
         and 4.00 pm to 7.00 pm

This enormous *art nouveau* metalic structure has had a chequered career since it was first commissioned by the Compañía Mexicana de Exposiciones Permanentes in 1903. The basic metal frame was built in Germany and shipped to Mexico in kit form. When it was first assembled on this site it acquired the nickname of Crystal Palace because of its ressemblance to the building of that name in London. When the Compañía Mexicana de Exposiciones Permanentes went into liquidation in 1905 the Chopo (named after the street on which it was first erected) passed into private ownership. In 1909 the building was rented by the government and was used to house the National Museum of Archeology, History and Ethnography. In 1910, during the centenary celebrations, it was rented to the Japanese delegation who used it to mount an exhibition of industrial art. The Chopo's second nickname, Japanese Pavillion, dates from that time.

It continued as a museum until 1964 when it was finally closed after several years of neglect. In 1973 extensive restoration was initiated, and in 1975 it reopened as the Chopo University Museum that we see today.

The Chopo hails from a period when architects were experimenting with steel structures and trying to balance the demands of functionalism with aesthetics. The Chopo achieves this balance where many others have not, and along with the better known Crystal Palace and Eiffel Tower, can be considered an outstanding aesthetic success.

Inside, the arched wooden roof and the bottle green glass that frames the windows combine to produce a Noah's Ark effect. Although there is a semi-permanent exhibition of the buildings history on the ground floor, the Chopo is now mainly used for temporary shows and other cultural events. It is well worth visiting, whether or not there is anything on display, if only to admire a building that has had a fascinating history and which manages to conjure up visions of fairy palaces and Victorian railway stations all at the same time.

Contemporary Art Cultural Center
Centro Cultural Arte Contemporáneo, A.C.

Campos Elíseos y Jorge Eliot, Col. Polanco   Map 3

Open: Tuesday to Sunday 10.00 am to 6.00 pm

This is Mexico's newest cultural center which was opened in 1986. It was built and financed by the country's largest private sector television and communications conglomerate, Televisa. The Televisa Cultural Foundation still runs and administers the center, thus providing an example of the important role that the private sector can play in a country's artistic and cultural life.

Its first use as a building was as the press and information center for the 1986 World Cup competition held in Mexico. It now divides its resources between permanent and temporary exhibitions and as a further education center for both young people and adults.

The Mexican architect Manuel Sordo Madaleno designed the building as a covered atrium of four storeys. The predominant building material is concrete of a *tezontle* color. For visitors staying in either the Presidente Chapultec or Nikko hotels, this center is but a stone's throw away, and well worth a visit. Apart from its several exhibitions, the center also has one of the most tasteful book and gift shops in the city.

The permanent exhibitions cover twentieth century modern paintings, photography and pre-Hispanic art. The photography collection, covering a complete history of this art form, is said to be one of the largest and most authoritative in the whole of Latin America.

The center also offers both day and evening extension programs in the fine arts and theatre. The facilities include a number of additional spaces that can be adapted for theatre, concerts, lectures and audiovisual presentations.

Cuicuilco Archeological Museum
El Museo Arqueologico de Cuicuilco

Insurgentes Sur s/n, Tlalpan   Map 6

Open: Tuesday to Sunday 10.00 am to 5.00 pm

Cuicuilco is a Nahuatl word meaning the place of singing and dancing. It was here, perhaps as long ago as the first millenium B.C., that an important ceremonial site was built with a massive, round pyramid as the center piece. Archeologists are still uncertain of the exact dates of Cuicuilco but it is possible that the site was populated several hundred years before the pyramid itself was constructed. Even so, the Cuicuilco pyramid is considered to be the oldest man-made structure on the North American continent. It was constructed on the central high plateau on the banks of what used to be the great lake that covered most of what is now the Valley of Mexico. The lake subsequently receded considerably leaving the area around Cuicuilco as dry land.

The construction of a pyramid of the Cuicuilco type presupposes the existence of well-developed, ritualistic cults. Findings at the site, which was first excavated in 1922, tell impressively of the people's attempt to come to terms with the forces of nature - forces which were eventually to destroy them. The museum contains several figurines representing female fertility, an important figure symbolic of the god of fire and the figure of a dog which represented a guide for the dead. On the top of the pyramid, which measures some twenty meters in height, are the remains of a ceremonial altar.

The core of the pyramid was made with clay mixed with stones. In fact, it is rather a truncated cone with a stone core. Lime was not used; and to prevent slippage in the huge structure, large rocks were inserted to form a fence-like protection. During excavation, human remains, fragments of pottery and the bases of simple domestic dwellings were uncovered. Judging from ceramic fragments, the monument was possibly erected in what is known as the higher pre-classic period (800 to 100 B.C.), but nothing is yet known for certain. What is known, however, is that in around 600 B.C. the Xitle volcano erupted and the cascading walls of molten lava completely destroyed the Cuicuilco site. In the museum there is a very dramatic and vividly imagined mural of this devastation by González Camarena. The lava from that vicious eruption of Xitle is still what gives the Pedregal de San Angel area its distinctive characteristics. Lava rock now forms the foundation of the whole area and continues to be the most commonly used material for building purposes.

The fear that these early inhabitants of Cuicuilco felt towards the divine forces of nature eventually proved to be well founded. An ancient Aztec poem, dedicated to the god of darkness and written long after the destruction of Cuicuilco, voices those same ancestral fears:

He mocks us
As He wishes, so He wills
He places us in the palm of His hand

He rolls us about,
Like pebbles, we roll and spin.
We make him laugh,
He mocks us.

The whole archeological site of Cuicuilco has recently been re-developed. From the entrance (the only access is from the slip road on Insurgentes Avenue traveling north), a number of walks have been landscaped, which provide a good introduction to the present day flora and fauna of the area. To the right, as one approaches the pyramid itself is a small, well-arranged museum. In two principal rooms, a fine collection of objects discovered on the site as well as maps, diagrams, chronological explanations and scale figures are displayed.

It is definitely worth climbing to the top of the pyramid with its view over another ceremonial site of modern times: the enormous Perisur shopping mall. From that spot, one can span several thousand years of human history. The volcanoes are less threatening than in the Cuicuilco era, but the vibrations from the same pressing need to make sense of our cosmic environment are still felt.

National Museum of Cultures
Museo Nacional de las Culturas

Calle Moneda 13, Col. Centro   Map1

Open: Tuesday to Saturday 9.00 am to 5.30 pm
            Sundays 9.00 am to 4.00 pm

The historic center of Mexico City is so rich in exquisite colonial buildings that sometimes the buildings themselves completely outshine anything that might be displayed within their walls.

Such is the case with this museum, housed in the old *Casa de Moneda,* or Royal Mint. The site itself goes back centuries. It was on this spot that Moctezuma had one of his palaces. It was here that he would retire to contemplate

Palette and brushes in Diego Rivera's Studio
Diego Rivera Studio Museum

affairs of state, its close proximity to the Templo Mayor presumably making divine inspiration more available to the Mexican monarch. When the ancient city of Tenochtitlán was parceled out after the conquest, the palace was given to Hernán Cortés who later sold it to the crown.

In 1729 the whole site, together with some adjoining buildings, were acquired by the Royal Mint for new premises. The first designs and constructions for the new Mint building were the work of Juan Peinado, but subsequent bickerings over technical defects and further modifications caused the project to be passed through several different hands. The building you see today dates from 1730. Over the years it has suffered its fair share of earthquake-related damage, including some nasty cracks in the major 1985 earthquake. However, it still survives as a jewel of colonial architecture. Humboldt, writing in the early nineteenth century, described it as, "the grandest and richest mint in the world."

The *Casa de Moneda* began its history as a museum in 1865 when the Emperor Maximilian ordered the Public Museum of Natural History, Archeology and History to be established in the building. However, since then, its various collections have been either re-classified or removed elsewhere. In 1940 it was called the National Museum of Anthropology until this, as well, moved on to better things in the newly opened museum of that name in Chapultepec Park. In 1965 it eventually settled on its present day title: the National Museum of Cultures.

To create a museum of world cultures was certainly an ambitious project. However, it would not be unfair to say that the present collection is perhaps more suited to schoolchildren than to the serious social anthropologist or archeologist. Prehistoric cultures, the ancient classical world, Russia, Africa, South East Asia, Japan, China and Europe are all represented in some form or another in some thirteen exhibition spaces. However the authorities will admit that the structure of the building does not lend itself ideally to these kinds of exhibits - the rooms are either too large or too small. Nevertheless, the modern use of this historic building is one of which Moctezuma would most likely have approved.

Diego Rivera Studio Museum
Museo Estudio Diego Rivera

Diego Rivera and Altavista, Col. San Angel Inn   Map 2

Open: Tuesday to Sunday 10.00 am to 6.00 pm

'Toad-Frog' was the title that Diego Rivera gave to his own self-portrait. In early twentieth century Mexican society he appeared as an outrageous and shocking rebel. After his death, however, he was almost immediately incorporated into one of the main arteries of Mexican cultural identity.

His studio house, built in 1933 by his architect friend Juan O'Gorman, seemed to most Mexicans at the time to be an exact reflection of the man. Even the bright blue in which it was painted must have assaulted the sedate, colonial structure of the nearby San Angel Inn (then a small, quiet hotel).

Diego Rivera commissioned this house to be his functional 'machine for living'. It was here that he lived with his young and beautiful third wife, painter Frida Kahlo, until she died in 1954. He continued to live in the house until his own death in 1957. Most of his large oil paintings and watercolors, almost all of the sketches for his large murals and many of his smaller, moveable murals were executed here.

On the ground floor there is a large room now mostly used for lectures. The further up one moves in the house, the closer one gets to its owner. An exhibition room on the first floor contains photographs, letters and documents. There is a chronological account of the painter's life (unfortunately only in Spanish) written by Raquél Tiból, the left wing art critic. The account explains the famous rift between Rivera and Siqueiros. The latter accused Rivera of having sold out, of being the official painter of the bourgeoisie and of having painted only fat, happy, smiling peasants.

Leaving this exhibition area with its several letters from Frida Kahlo (many decorated with pressed flowers and one signed with a lipstick kiss), and going upstairs, one comes to the main attraction: Diego Rivera's studio. One wall is all window. His big easel dominates the room. Many of the paintings here are on loan, few actually belong to the museum. Hanging from the ceiling are his famous Judas figures and

Cupola of El Carmen
Museum of El Carmen

papier-maché painted skeletons and monsters. Among the usual artist's clutter is some of Rivera's collection of pre-Hispanic and popular art pieces, displayed on plain, wooden shelves. Rivera preferred to use simple rustic Mexican furniture at a time when most well-to-do Mexicans were buying foreign designs.

His bedroom is on the same floor as his studio. This is small and cabin-like, just large enough for his hospital bed with its brightly colored hand-woven bedspread. This reduced bedroom space underlines Rivera's Bauhausian, functional belief that houses should be machines for living; but sleeping, in that scheme of things, was not allotted much space! A few of his hand-painted walking sticks still stand in the cupboard.

The house is in fact made up of two sets of quarters joined together by an overhead bridge. The original idea was to provide a set of 'his' and 'hers' quarters arranged separately. Frida's part of the house is not open to the public. The focus is more on the painter and his work rather than on how the house functioned domestically.

There are some fascinating video tapes available for viewing on request (parts of the original film were taken in this house with the painter in residence). There is a small, well-stocked bookshop on the premises. Diego Rivera's Studio Museum makes an excellent stop before or after a visit to the next door San Angel Inn for lunch.

Museum of El Carmen
Museo de El Carmen

Avenida Revolución 4 and 6, Col. San Angel Inn   Map 2

Open: Monday to Sunday 10.00 am to 5.00 pm

On a busy corner of Revolución street in San Angel, opposite the local municipal offices, stands this superb colonial monastery. Many passers by mistake it for just another church and walk on unenlightened - the lack of suitable signs does El Carmen a serious disservice. Built between 1615 and 1628, the monks benefitted from the services of Friar Andrés de San Miguel who was not only a skilled architect but also an expert in hydro-dynamics and astronomy. To capture both the spirit and the grandeur of the place one has to imagine how it was: landscaped in extensive grounds which comprised majestic gardens and plentiful orchards of peach, cherry and pear trees. Fresh mountain streams watered the vegetable gardens and flowers, and olive trees grew alongside the graceful aqueducts which stretched down from San Angel to Copilco and Coyoacan. Everything, it must have seemed then, conspired to encourage contemplation. For centuries this monastic complex was a center of economic, artistic and social interest. Today, it still stands as one of the finest monuments to early colonial Mexico.

The main buildings open to the public, which cover the church, cloister, sacristy, refectory, cells and community chapel, are all intact and in passable condition. In fact, two Carmelite priests are still in residence here.

From in front of the church, you enter the museum to the right and then turn left into the sunny cloisters, with a Puebla-glazed, blue-tiled fountain in the central patio. Above can be seen the spectacular tiled cupola and belfry. A small door leads to the sacristy with its painted stucco ceiling and heavy ancient furniture. The room is dominated by an imposing ecclesiastical chest of drawers at the far end used for vestments. Five large oils by Cristobál de Villalpando treat mysterious religious scenes. Perhaps today, like the ancient Mexican codices, the modern visitor needs more explanation of the religious symbolism so vibrant and common centuries ago. El Carmen falls down in this explanation category: there is none, and visitors are left to guess too much.

Just off the sacristy is a large washroom with five of the original blue and white tiled basins. A feast for the ceramics lover. From here, wide stone steps lead down to the crypt. The exquisite tiled altars are decorated with leaf and flower designs in ochre, emerald green and shades of blue. The money for this larger-than-normal crypt came from Don Juan de Ortega y Baldivici, a pious soldier and businessman whose generosity ensured that he and his family could go to their final rest in a holy place. In 1970, a team of anthropologists, investigating the burial site below the floor, found that it had been systematically ransacked over a long period of time. Perhaps the Zapatista troops, who lodged in the building

Figure of Virgin (XIII century)
Franz Mayer Museum

briefly, had a hand in this. Mummified bodies from these graves are still on rather macabre display today. It is likely that some accidental combination of the humidity and soil composition caused the mummification process. Whatever the case, their presence still causes some heated arguments both for and against a proper re-burial.

Upstairs, a typical Carmelite cell and a small gilded chapel have been beautifully preserved. Outside, only the faintest remnant of the once sumptious gardens remains - the strolling, prayerful friars are gone.

No visitor to the city should miss seeing El Carmen. Its ancient, sacred areas still speak of the Mexico of three centuries ago. A fascinating building, obviously suffering from a lack of conservation funds, and therefore maintained patchwork style.

Franz Mayer Museum
Museo Franz Mayer

Av. Hidalgo 45, Col. Centro   Map 1

Open: Tuesday to Sunday 10.00 am to 5.00 pm

New York has its Guggenheim, London has its Courtauld. Now Mexico City has its Franz Mayer, which is set fair to become one of the most important and prestigious museums in the Americas. The formula is a well tried one: rich collector-industrialist, good financial backing (in this case a trust administered by the National Bank of Mexico), strong support from the local city government, a well-trained, professional and dedicated staff and you get a museum that is comparable to the best in the world.

Opened in 1986, and still in the process of refining and amplifying its facilities, the Franz Mayer museum is one of the most impressive outgrowths of the restoration program of the *centro histórico* in downtown Mexico City. The old ruins of the Women's Hospital (dating originally from the seventeenth century) were chosen as the fundamental shell for the new, modern and dynamic Franz Mayer. The architectural work combined restoration of an original colonial monument with creative and innovative adaptions to produce a museum that was designed to fill a yawning gap in the cultural infrastructure of the nation. There is no doubt that the Franz Mayer project has been a resounding success.

This is an art museum with a marked emphasis on the applied arts. It stretches credibility to think that all the contents of this fine museum used to be in Mayer's house in Las Lomas. The appeal to all the senses is immediate: the smell of old wood and warm stone, the dazzling glimpse of precious metals, the lacquered furniture, glazed pottery and silken tapestries transport one into another world. The place is a treasure house, and the world is Mexican cultural history - in a gilded nutshell.

If there is a theme running through the Franz Mayer, apart from its eclecticism, it is that Mexican culture was radically transformed by colonialization. However, far from selling out to their conquerors, the dexterity of the indigenous artists and artesans allowed them to adapt and absorb the newly imported cultural elements and produce particular styles of their own. In the gallery of talavera pottery, for example, one can see how styles brought from Spanish possessions in the Orient were absorbed and transformed by local artists into new, peculiarly Mexican expressions.

The museum is rich in *objets d'art*, furniture, ceramics, textiles, gold and silver work, painting and sculpture. Mayer was one of those collectors who dedicated his entire life to the careful acquisition of pieces based on his own extensive knowledge and a fine understanding of the historic and artistic mixture. Throughout the museum, good taste combines with noteworthy labelling to produce some commendable displays. Also of note is the very agreeable effect of playing recorded classical music in the background in all the exhibition rooms. This simply accentuates the sophisticated atmosphere of the Franz Mayer.

In the not-to-be-missed category here is the superb collection (one of the few in existence) of *talavera poblana*. The Mayer is also well stocked with some fine paintings from the Spanish, French, Italian and Dutch schools including a work by Francisco Zubarán. For sheer elegance, the black-walled gold and silver room with only spotlights to pick out the objects in the showcases is difficult to fault. The effect is extraordinarily dramatic and beautiful.

*A corner of the Franz Mayer Museum
with antique clock*

The Franz Mayer is a fine museum and the result of some very enterprising teamwork led by its director, Maestro Eugenio Sisto. It should be on the top of most people's lists when planning a visit to the downtown area of Mexico City.

Frida Kahlo Museum
Museo Frida Kahlo

Londres 247, Coyoacán   Map 4

Open: Tuesday to Sunday 10.00 am to 2.00 pm
        & 3.00 pm to 6.00 pm

Frida Kahlo was born in this house on July 6, 1907, the third daughter of Guillermo and Matilde Kahlo. Her father, from a Hungarian Jewish family, had come to Mexico only sixteen years before. Her mother was Mexican and she was given the names Magdalena Carmen Frida so that she could be baptized with a christian name. Her third name, the one her family used, means 'peace' in German. Unfortunately, peace was not a blessing that would accompany her throughout her short life of forty-seven years.

The large house, which was built by Frida's father, is made of gray volcanic rock and painted cobalt blue with *tezontle* bordering and green for the ironwork. It has a cold, stern, almost forbidding atmosphere about it which is not what one expects. Somehow one pictures Frida in a house with much more sunlight. She and Diego Rivera lived here from 1929 until Frida's death in 1954.

When Frida was six years-old she was stricken with polio and only with sheer determination and gruelling exercise was she able to overcome her disability. Twelve years later, tragedy struck again. Frida was involved in a street car accident in which her her body, from one side to the other at the level of the pelvis, was punctured by a steel handrail. It was an accident of the type to make one recoil with horror. Her spinal column had been broken in three places together with her collarbone and two ribs. Her right leg had eleven fractures and her right foot was dislocated and crushed. Her left shoulder was out of joint and her pelvis broken in three places. The handrail had pierced her body at the level of the abdomen. She had to suffer at least thirty-two operations, and was literally tortured by a series of surgical apparati supposed to help her damaged spine. One such plaster corset is on show in the museum, painted all over with floral designs, giving us an insight into Frida's black humor.

From 1925 onwards, her life was one long battle against decay. As the writer Andrés Henestrosa commented, "Frida lived dying." But even when close to death, drugged with morphine, she still managed to appear at an exhibition of her paintings, lying dramatically in a four-poster bed in the gallery, receiving her friends in grand theatrical style. Her last, unfinished painting, *My Family*, can be seen in the museum.

Frida began painting after her accident, lying in bed with a specially-made easel propped up in front of her. For self portraits she used a mirror hung directly above her bed which can also be seen here. Art became one of the mainstays of her life, the other being her husband, Diego Rivera. They married, he for the third time, in the Coyoacán Town Hall on August 21, 1929.

Unlike her husband, Frida did not achieve fame as a painter in her lifetime. While Diego's work was commanding high prices in auction houses all over the world, Frida's paintings were admired by only a small circle of intimate friends. Diego certainly recognized and encouraged his wife's talents, and they had an enormous respect for each other as artists. Today, Frida Kahlo has become a well-known figure, respected internationally for her artistic talent as well as for her unique approach to life and death. Many of her paintings, photographs and scenes of her everyday life that are exhibited in this museum speak of how, through her painting, she was able to project her suffering out of herself and onto canvas. The result is strange, touching and intensely disturbing.

But life did have a brighter side for Frida. With Diego, she traveled extensively, always astoundingly attired in her exotic Mexican folk dresses (many are still hanging here). Dressed in her Tehuana costume, Frida would cause much astonishment in the street when she traveled abroad. Once, after leaving a bank in New York, a little boy who had seen her, asked, "where's the circus?" such was the larger-than-life impression that she made. Frida and Diego both found it

Frida Kahlo

irresistable to act outrageously, scandalising Mexican polite society in the thirties and forties.

When she was well enough, Frida gave art classes, and her students remember how she made her pupils into a family and her house into an exotic home for them. Perhaps her pupils helped her to keep one of the greatest sorrows of her life at bay: her inability to bear a child. Her one miscarriage is depicted over and over again in a series of heart rending canvasses, several of which can be seen in the museum.

When Frida died, Diego Rivera donated this house to the nation in memory of his wife. In the museum is one of her bedroom cushions touchingly embroidered with an appeal to the man she loved: *No me olvides amor mío* (Do not forget me my love).

Her family home-turned-museum, which now preserves so many of her personal belongings, a large number of her paintings and a great part of the couple's collection of art treasures stands in remembrance of one of the most complex, yet inspiring Mexican artists of this century. Apart from a fine collection of her own work on display here (which includes an arresting self-portrait done in charcoal in 1952), there are some marvellous small oils by Clausell, an extensive collection of ex-votos on the staircase, and a fairy tale blue and yellow kitchen to enjoy. One of the most moving parts of the tour through the house is to climb the stairs and enter Frida's studio - there, in front of the easel with its unfinished portrait is her wheelchair. The courage of this woman who managed to live such an intensely provocative and creative life is almost beyond comprehension. She has a place in Mexico's cultural history that will never be usurped.

Geles Cabrera Museum of Sculpture
Museo Escultórico Geles Cabrera

Avenida Xicoténcatl 181, Coyoacán   Map 4

Open: Monday to Friday 10.00 am to 1.00 pm
          and 5.00 pm to 7.00 pm

Geles Cabrera was born in Mexico in 1930. She is one of the most renowned woman sculptors in the country. Some of her works are in the museum of Modern Art in Mexico City (see entry) as well as in museums in Israel and Bulgaria. However, this level of exposure in museums appeared not to be sufficient for the artist; hence this private collection-turned-museum which she created. As she herself says, "I wanted to make a museum here in Coyoacán - a little corner where people could come and sit and enjoy my work." Admirable sentiments in a sense, although owners of small private museums should realize that there is more to making a museum than just putting a sign up outside your front door; which in this case often appears to be locked during advertised opening times! However, she is in good company with the Frida Kahlo Museum (see entry) just around the comer, and the two locations can easily be combined on the same visit.

Plastic arts are often notoriously difficult to evaluate, especially for the lay person. One is sometimes left with the suspicion that there is a lot of artistic hyperbole in modern sculpture. But, for the I-know-what-I-like school, there is a lot to choose from in Cabrera's work. The creative outpouring has been steady over a number of years and her use of media is eclectic. She works in stone, bronze, fiber, terracota and scrap iron. One of her more recent forrays has been into newspaper sculpture which is an interesting development.

Geology Museum of the UNAM

Museo de Geología
de la Universidad Nacional Autónoma de
México

Jaime Torres Bodet 176,   Map 5
Col. Santa María la Ribera

Open: Tuesday to Sunday 10.00 am to 5.00 pm

This neo-classic building, which was formerly the National Geological Institute (inaugurated by Porfirio Díaz in 1886), is nothing short of magnificent. The facade of the building is exquisite and particularly noteworthy are the *art nouveau* stained-glass windows and copper-forged railings. The style is a wonderful example of what was in vogue during the Porfirio Díaz era in Mexico.

Inside are the usual minerals, rocks and fossils - not necessarily in that order. However, they do have some important works by the Mexican landscape painter, José María Velasco. The collection will probably appeal more to the geologist on holiday than the average visitor, but it does merit a quick detour to admire the building itself.

Guadalupe Basilica Museum
Museo de la Basílica de Guadalupe

Villa de Guadalupe

Open: Tuesday to Sunday 10.00 am to 6.00 pm

Millions of pilgrims visit Guadalupe every year. It is certainly the most venerated Christian shrine in Mexico, and ranks with Lourdes and Fatima as an important world center of

Marian devotion. The story of the apparitions of the Blessed Virgin to Juan Diego in 1531 shows remarkable similarity of form to those of Fatima and Lourdes.

On December 9, 1531, an indian named Juan Diego was on his way to mass at the church of Santiago Tlateloco. As he was walking along the side of Tepeyac hill he heard music and a woman, radiating a great light, suddenly appeared before him. The lady requested that a place of worship be built there on the hill, and she asked Juan Diego to relay this request to Juan de Zumárraga, the then Bishop of Mexico.

Juan Diego dutifully carried out this mission but only encountered disbelief on behalf of the ecclesiastical authorities who reproached him for being superstitious. When Diego returned to the hill, he saw the lady once more and reported to her what had happened. She told him to press her request a second time, and on the following day, Diego went again to see the bishop. This time he was questioned more closely. Although Juan de Zumárraga still had his doubts, he was beginning to be swayed by the peasant's tale. He asked that the Lady of the apparition send him some proof of her identity.

Once more Juan Diego returned to the place where he had first seen the Lady and explained to her what had happened. She replied that the bishop would be given his proof. On December 12, Juan Diego's uncle awoke very ill and Juan Diego was despatched to find a priest. Again the Lady appeared to him and reassured him that his uncle would recover. She asked Juan Diego to go and pick some flowers at the top of Tepeyac hill. Although out of season, the indian had no difficulty in finding plenty of roses on the hill. He picked them and brought them to the lady who touched the flowers and said that he was to take them to the bishop as proof.

Juan Diego gathered up the roses in his tunic and hurried off to seek an audience with the bishop. When he was in front of Juan de Zumárraga he unfolded his tunic and the roses fell to the floor. There, miraculously emblazoned on his peasant's smock for all to see, was the image of the Blessed Virgin. The bishop and everyone present immediately knelt in wonder and amazement.

The image imprinted on the coarse cloth of Juan Diego's tunic was taken at once to the bishop's private chapel and held there until the hermitage requested by the Blessed Virgin was constructed.

Today, on top of Tepeyac hill, there is a small chapel supposedly on one of the sites where the Lady had appeared to Juan Diego. At the bottom of the hill in a huge square are the Old Basilica (dating from 1536), the Church of the Capuchines directly to one side of the Old Basilica (dating from 1789) and the New Basilica which was opened in 1976. Today, the image of Our Lady of Guadalupe is venerated over the high altar of the New Basilica. It is a very compelling and hauntingly beautiful testimonial to a series of apparitions that occured over four hundred years ago. The image of the Blessed Virgin is of a dark-skinned lady radiating light. It is to this shrine that millions of devout worshippers come every year. As the Virgin of Guadalupe had said to Juan Diego, she wanted a place of worship built on this spot so that She could hear and relieve the sufferings of all her children.

The Guadalupe Basilica Museum is housed in part of the Old Basilica. This is in such a state of disrepair due to earthquake damage and earth subsidence, that most of it is closed to the public. The entrance to the museum is found on the left side of the basilica near the steps that lead up to the top of Tepeyac hill.

One enters a long gallery on whose walls are an extraordinarily fine collection of retablos or ex-votos. These primitive paintings done to a standard size on tin and, in more recent times, on cardboard, are a very typical Mexican genre of thanksgiving pictures. They are executed by the beneficiary of a miraculous intervention which has caused the recovery from a serious illness or the avoidance of an accident or for favors granted. They all follow a distinct primitive composition: The Blessed Virgin, the supplicant and a small motif of the illness or whatever is the content of the retablo. They are classic expressions of popular religious art and have a simplicity and directness which is very moving. In recent years, many of these retablos have been disappearing from churches and shrines throughout the country only to reappear in private collections. By contrast, it is a joy to find such a large collection of them still in their intended place. They are votive offerings to be hung in churches, not in a private sitting room.

From this gallery, one enters the huge sacristy, with a dominating canvas by an anonymous artist depicting the placing of the image of the Virgin of Guadalupe and the first miracle.

From the sacristy, there is an entrance to the only chapel of the Old Basilica open to the public. This has a magnificent choir screen of worked metal and wood and some sumptious blue and gold mosaics in the recesses.

The major part of this collection is found in the rooms above the sacristy. A spectacular staircase leads to this area. Religious paintings from the seventeenth and eighteenth centuries dominate. Many are by unknown artists but there are some fine works by Cabrera, Villalpando and Juan Cordero's *The Redeemer and the Woman Taken in Adultery* painted in 1853.

One or two of the more outstanding pieces in this museum include Tiburcio Miranda's colored wood carvings, an ivory statute of St Michael the Archangel and a Holy Family arrangement also in ivory. These last pieces originated in the Philippines and came to Mexico via the Chinese trading ships.

National Museum of History
Museo Nacional de Historia

Chapultepec Castle, Col. Bosque de Chapultepec   Map 3

Open: Tuesday to Sunday 9.00 am to 5.00 pm

Castles on tops of hills are the stuff of which fairy tales are made. Chapultepec hill, on which the present castle stands, is not only one of the most famous hills in the world but it is also one of the traditional symbols of Mexican patriotism. Stories about the hill evoke that same 'once upon a time' feel that we normally associate with ancient fables. For it was here, once upon a time, that the rain god, Tlaloc, had his sanctuary. Many earthen and stone objects made in his honor have been found on Chapultepec hill. Later, the Aztec emperors chose the hill as the site for their summer residences. Its royal pedigree is long and illustrious.

After the conquest, the site became the official residence of the viceroys, although few of them made great use of it. In fact it was not until Emperor Maximilian came on the scene (1864-1867) that Chapultepec Castle came back into

Hand-painted miniature of national emblem
National Museum of History

its own. Maximilian renovated the almost ruined buildings and made the castle his offical residence. The castle that you see today is basically his creation. After the fall of the empire, it again fell into disuse, but its obvious attraction did not escape the attention of Porfirio Díaz (1876-1911) who again turned the castle into an official government residence. Finally, in 1939, President Lázaro Cárdenas decreed that it become the National History Museum and it was inaugurated as such in 1944.

National history museums (of any country) are notoriously difficult to appreciate. This one is no exception. The great variety of totally diverse objects that make up its collection can be unsettling to the visitor who knows little of the details of Mexican history. Mexican history, in any case, tends to be confusing at the best of times. Here, displayed in Chapultec Castle, are the paraphernalia that really do make up history. Flags, cannons, coaches, baroque furniture, paintings, uniforms, photos, documents, silver and gold ware and coins are the sort of exhibits that will greet you after a fifteen minute walk up from Chapultepec Park below. Unfortunately, there is no elevator. The walk up is probably best started from the car park at the Museum of Modern Art. But, once on the castle terraces, one can enjoy a magnificent view of the Paseo de la Reforma (another of Maximilian's projects) which makes all that trudging up hill well worthwhile. The view really does merit the not-to-be-missed notice.

Assuming you have made it to the top and that Tlaloc has not drenched you, there are many things to be admired. Perhaps most notable are the many fine murals by Orozco, Siqueiros, O'Gorman, Camarena and Bolivar. The borderline in Mexico between history itself and mural painting (which has been so well represented throughout the country) is often less than clearly drawn. Murals are never more than interpretations of historical events according to contemporary politics and the ideas and ideals of the artists themselves.

Other important items in this extensive collection include the famous Miguel Cabrera portrait of Sor Juana Inés de la Cruz. Note the painter's humorous touch of making the nun-poetess mark the place in the book she is reading with her finger. Other fine paintings include some mid-eighteenth century scenes of everyday life and a few excellent landscapes. There is also a large and important collection of miniatures painted on a variety of metals and ivory. Apart from the paintings, the museum contains some interesting historical documents and some stunning maps. One of the latter, supposedly drawn by Hernán Cortés, is a work of art and another by Alonso Santa Cruz (1555) shows an early plan of Mexico City complete with ships and boats on the lake.

Sadly, the museum's enthusiasm for Mexican history can result in often delicate and beautiful objects being lumped together under large didactic slogans (e.g. 'The Fight against the Dictatorship'). However, the same lustiness does not extend into the overall upkeep and maintenance of the museum and its grounds. Some of fountains have no water; the gardens have no flowers to speak of and many of the flower pots (painted institutional red over natural clay) often only contain moribund geraniums. This is a pity. It is all a far cry from the ancient Aztec summer residence.

Museums do serve to illustrate history in its turbulent progress, but after a visit to Chapultepec Castle, one could be left with the impression of having been abandoned in the pages of a history textbook. Those of us who need guidance find there is no teacher to answer all those legitimate questions.

Gallery of the National Museum of History (Snail Museum)
Galería del Museo Nacional de Historia (Museo Caracol)

Chapultepec Castle, Col. Bosque de Chapultepec   Map 3

Open: Tuesday to Sunday 9.00 am to 5.00 pm

This has a most confusing series of titles. It is more commonly known as the Snail Museum because of the intriguing snail- like shape of the building. However, it is in fact a gallery attached to the National Museum of History in Chapultepec Castle (see entry), and it is located just a few yards down from the castle entrance. It is also called the Museum of the

Lucha del Pueblo Mexicano por su Libertad (Fight of the Mexican People for their Liberty) which is the gallery's theme.

The building was inaugurated in 1960 by then-President Lopez Mateos as a purpose-built museum designed by Pedro Ramirez Vázquez. Entering from the road that leads to Chapultepec Castle, one is beginning at the top of the building. The exhibition rooms then follow a descending ramp built around a central domed tower. As the descending ramps are circular in design, it is easy to understand why the snail nickname is so appropriate.

The museum covers the period from the last years of the viceroyalty in Mexico (1800 - 1810) to the enacting of the 1917 Constitution. The space is divided into twelve chronological sections each given a title. The idea was to tell the story of Mexico's growth towards full independence in a series of didactic sequences spread throughout twelve rooms. Certain techniques and exhibition aids are consistently and successfully used to achieve this purpose. Specially commissioned paintings, maps (particularly well used to illustrate journeys and battles), photographs and three-dimensional models are cleverly used to bring a long and often complicated story to life.

The whole effect, which is supplemented by wall texts, can be likened to walking through a well-illustrated history book with the added advantage of meeting the principal protagonists in their real-life model settings. Certain of these creations, like the execution of the Emperor Maximilian or Madero's arrival in Mexico City in 1911, are brilliantly executed and quickly fire the imagination.

One can easily spend an hour and a half meandering through the Snail Museum, and it is a popular museum for families with school-age children. For them it is a well-presented and entertaining history lesson and much to be recommended to anyone interested in Mexico's development as a nation since 1800.

After the last exhibition room, the ramp ends at the foot of the interior tower. This final space contains a facsimile of the 1917 Constitution in a silver casket at the base of Mexican national emblem sculpted in the modern style by José Chávez Morado.

National Museum of Interventions
Museo Nacional de las Intervenciones

20 de agosto y General Anaya
Col. Churubusco   Map 4

Open: Tuesday to Sunday 9.00 am to 6.00 pm

A strange one this. A museum dedicated to interventions (armed invasions might be a better term) might not be on everyone's hit parade of museum themes. Add to that the location of this collection - an ancient seventeenth century convent - and one's sense of perplexity increases. On first thought they make strange bedfellows, but in fact it was in this monastery, on August 20, 1847, that Mexican troops put up a spirited but unsuccessful defense against the invading U.S. troops. Under the leadership of General Anaya, and with the help of some Irish deserters from the U.S. side, they fought to the last round of ammunition.

The Mexican psyche is understandably obsessed with armed interventions from outside powers. The conquest itself was traumatic, and even after independence from Spain (1821), the Spaniards attempted a reconquest of Mexico with Isidro Barradas (1829). The French had a go in 1838 and again in 1862 and, in the intervening period, Mexico fought a war (1846-1848) with the U.S.A. In 1914 and 1916, U.S. troops also launched unwanted forrays into Mexican territory. This museum documents these interventions with a clever pastiche of documents, records, memorabilia and a miscellany of period objects (both social and military) which add up to a chronological and thematic display of these unwanted incursions on Mexican sovereignty.

The design of the museum prefers to let people draw their own conclusions. Nothing is rammed down the throat, although the emphasis throughout is more on the 'brave, patriotic Mexicans' rather than on the villany of the aggressors. Any descendents of the invaders (be they Spanish, French or North American) would not be offended in any way by the museum's contents. From the inoffensive looking cannons flanking the outside entrance, the historical and social contents blend pleasantly. Just the right amount of well-

National Museum of Interventions

cared for items displayed according to the shape and size of the rooms. The whole adds up to a glorious still life of furniture and objects.

It is difficult not to be distracted by the beauty of the convent building and gardens themselves. The painted stonework of the convent has been exquisitely restored (there is a school of restoration in the grounds) and the re-painted motifs on the pillars are a fine example of pre-Hispanic patterns being used in a colonial religious building. There are several curves and rectangles, seen the one through the other, to be enjoyed; and bright, recessed windows each with its own special view. From the exhibition rooms one can view an old fig tree, a minute patio overgrown with bougainvillia with gray stone walls and trees behind. The bell towers, fountains and the crumbling stone of a pinkish cupola all combine to create an enchanting oasis of tranquility. One expects the objects related to war to clash with their surroundings - perhaps their very juxtaposition cunningly makes the point of the whole display.

On entering the convent to the right is a walled orchard with a fountain set in to the far wall. On leaving the museum area to the left is a geometrical, flowered garden where, in the dappled shade of the jacaranda trees one is left to contemplate the scars left on a country by violent interventions. The social scars, mainly Spanish and French, are equally well documented at this museum which is highly recommended for both the casual and the serious historian.

Art Gallery of the Church of la Profesa
Pinacoteca de la Iglesia de La Profesa

Isabel La Católica y Madero
Col. Centro   Map 1

Open: Sunday 12.00pm to 2.00 pm

This impressive collection of paintings has only recently been reopened after a seven year period of restoration. Visiting times for the public are currently limited to two hours on Sundays, but the importance of the gallery should not be understated.

La Profesa dates from 1720 and was the headquarters of the Jesuit order until they were expelled from Mexico (and from the entire Spanish Empire) in 1767. In 1771 the church was taken over by the Oratorians, an order of secular priests founded by St Philip Neri in Rome in 1575.

Access to the museum galleries is via a door to the right of the main altar. Stairs lead up to the first of these, while the second level is gained by climbing more twisted stairs past grilled windows with nesting pigeons to a space by the organ loft. There is that rather exciting feeling of being in a forbidden place above a church, rather like mice in wainscotting!

This is a priceless collection of Mexican religious painting from the sixteenth to the nineteenth centuries. It was amassed over the years by both the religious orders associated with La Profesa. There are some four hundred and fifty pictures, the bulk of which were painted by artists during the viceregal period of Mexican history. Apart from fine work by Cristóbal de Villalpando, Juan Correo and the famous Rodríquez family (generations of painters both male and female), there are some arresting examples of early anonymous meditations on life and death in the *Casa de Ejercicios* room.

Guided tours are given by the Oratorian priests every Sunday, and although this is not an easy museum to find, it makes a fascinating pre-lunch outing if one is exploring the downtown historic center of Mexico City.

Leon Trotsky monument
Leon Trotsky Museum

Leon Trotsky Museum
Museo León Trotsky

Viena 45, Coyoacán   Map 4

Open: Tuesday to Friday 10.00 am to 2.00 pm and 3.00 pm
      to 5.30 pm. Saturday and Sunday 10.30 am to 4.00 pm

It was in this house, on May 24th 1936, that Siqueiros and twenty followers burst into Trotsky's bedroom in an unsuccessful assasination attempt. The bullet holes are still there as testimony. From that date on, Trotsky became justifiably paranoid, and closed up most of the windows and doors to half their size. Trotsky originally chose the house (which dates from 1903) when he came to live in Mexico precisely for its fortress-like characteristics. The threats against his life from his Stalinist pursuers were always real. He calculated that its high-walled exterior and its three towers would provide him with an impregnable defense. In the end, he was wrong. The successful assasination, with a pick axe, eventually came on August 20, 1940. Román Mercadel was a Spanish agent of the Soviet secret police. He had successfully managed to worm his way into the affections of Trotsky's secretary, and thus he was able to gain access to the fortress. Trotsky was killed while at work at his desk. The books he was actually reading when killed are on display in the house.

Trotsky's bedroom, study, dining room and other living areas of the house are open to the public. Everything is sparse, as it was in Trotsky's time. He hated adornments, and was content with only the barest essentials, with books being an abundant exception. The latter are in several languages. Trotsky was a polyglot and spoke Russian, English, German, Spanish, Yiddish, Ukrainian and French. The wooden floors still retain their original painted red coloring. There is a fascinating collection of photographs dotted around the house showing Trotsky in the company of many a famous figure in the Mexico of the thirties. The museum also contains a bust of Trotsky (executed by a cousin of Winston Churchill) and Juan O'Gorman's Trotsky monument in the garden. The ashes of both Trotsky and his wife (who died in Paris in

1962) are buried under this monument. Overall, the atmosphere inclines towards a cold and faded page of history.

Trotsky's wife lived here until 1961. Her art books and meticulously kept household accounts are still on view. It was Trotsky's grandson who eventually turned the house into a museum in 1962. He had lived in the house with his grandparents and witnessed the assasination. Daniel Bolado, the resident caretaker of the museum, offers visitors (mostly non-Mexicans) a sensitive, low-key but lucid tour. His facts he has first hand from the grandson and, in true Trotsky tradition, can manage quite a number of languages.

This is definitely a no-frills museum, but one that will strongly appeal to Trotsky aficionados. Unfortunately, there is little mileage here for serious researchers, as Leon Trotsky sent all his notes and papers to Harvard University before his death.

Marine Grotto
Gruta Marina

Atlantis Marine Park   Map 3
3a Sección del Bosque de Chapultepec

Open: Tuesday to Sunday 10.30 am to 5.30 pm

This can only be visited by paying the entrance fee to the Atlantis Marine Park. However, the one ticket is also good for the dolphin and seal acquarium show which is featured at regular intervals throughout the day.

The man-made grotto, complete with stalactites, was conceived of as didactic space for children to learn about the importance of the sea, marine life and the dangers of pollution. In such a small space (three rooms), it is difficult to do more than just skim the surface of such a large subject. Young children will find the displays enjoyable and interesting. The fish tanks are well arranged against painted backdrops and contain some thirty or so specimens. Sandwiched between two fish tanks is one that contains only man's debris (beer bottles and plastic tubing etc) which makes the point about contaminating the marine environment with considerable impact.

Other exhibits include charts, maps and several fish skeletons, with the final touch left until the exit - a whale's cranium!

Luis Márquez Romay Museum of Mexican Clothing

Museo de la Indumentaria Mexicana Luis Márquez Romay

José Ma. Izazaga 80, Col. Centro   Map 1

Open: Tuesday to Sunday 9.00 am to 6.00 pm

One of the most important expressions of popular Mexican culture is to be found in the great variety of traditional costumes that still abound in this country. This fascinating museum, which opened in 1985, would not have been possible without the dedication of Luis Márquez Romay (1899-1978) who amassed this priceless collection of Mexican regional clothing.

Márquez was originally a prize-winning photographer who began to investigate and document Mexican folklore. Amazed and impressed by its richness, Márquez soon became a major collector of *indumentaria* (the word rather defies an adequate translation) as well as continuing to record details of local fiestas and other aspects of indigenous everyday life. He was a friend of all the great Mexican personalities of his time and in 1977 he donated his collection to the Claustro de Sor Juana A.C. with the purpose of founding this museum.

Downstairs is a permanent collection of his photographs. Everyday objects, parties and portraits are all depicted but the main emphasis is always on the dress or headgear.

On the second floor is the bulk Márquez's collection of traditional Mexican clothes. Due to the fragility of the exhibits, the costumes are constantly rotated, and there is a workshop on the same premises which does a fine job in maintaining and restoring them. However, the visitor can always be sure of seeing several *china poblana* costumes which delight with the sheer exuberance of their designs. The number of explanations and even legends as to the origin of this curious dress would fill a complete book in themselves. They all have the charm of an antique patchwork: lots of ribbons, often a waist-coat over a usually white blouse, and always a shawl. The skirt, over a lace petticoat, never fails to be anything less than extravagent with its scalloped hems, insets of all kinds of material and lots of sequins.

Regional costumes from Chiapas and Oaxaca are particulary well represented here as are antique items of clothing. This a well-run museum which will delight photographers and costume enthusiasts alike. It also provides a useful yardstick for anyone who wishes to buy genuine ethnic garments in the many markets that sell this type of clothing. The overall picture is one of bright colors, elaborate weaving techniques and beautiful embroidery, all of which are the hallmarks of the indian clothing of Mexico.

Museum of the History of Mexican Medicine

Museo de la Historia de la Medicina Mexicana

Brasil 33, Col. Centro   Map 6

Open: Monday to Friday 10.00 am to 6.00 pm

The museums of Mexico City continue to delight with unintentional anomalies and humorous juxtapositions. Here, in what was the old Palace of the Inquisition, is a museum dedicated to the history of medical practices in Mexico! The cure for heresy during the period of the Inquisition (1569-1820) was certainly far from herbal. For the minor heretical ailments, a slight scorching was often prescribed while for the more intractable conditions, involuntray combustion was not without precedent. Under such circumstances, it is sometimes difficult to appreciate the accusations of barbarism that the Spanish conquerors brought forth when describing Aztec religious practices!

Cultural comparisons aside, this museum is worth visiting if only to admire Pedro de Arrieta's magnificent Tribunal building. The Tribunal of the Inquisition had been located on this site since 1569, but the present building dates from 1732. The facade, adorned on both sides by four columns, is placed on the corner of the building. The coat of arms of the Inquisition was placed above the richly-decorated main entrance. Inside, the monumental stairway is impressive.

From 1855 until 1956 the building was used by the School of Medicine of the university. After its restoration in 1976, it retained its medical connections and now houses a ten-roomed museum containing documents, instruments, books and paintings illustrative of Mexican medical practice from pre-Hispanic times onward.

Mexico City Museum
Museo de la Ciudad de México

Pino Suárez 30, Col. Centro   Map 1

Open: Tuesday to Sunday 9.30 am to 7.30 pm

For anyone interested in the historic center of Mexico City, a visit to this old palatial residence of the Counts of Santiago Calimaya is not to be missed. It was one of the early palaces of Colonial Mexico dating from 1558. However, it was extensively remodelled in 1779 by the Mexican architect Francisco Guerrero y Torres. It is a wonderfully fine example of a baroque residence of the viceregal period. Before entering the museum, which was inaugurated in 1964, it is worth standing on the opposite side of the street to admire the perfect proportions and colors of the palace. Many of the stones used in its foundations and base probably came from the Great Aztec Temple. In fact, on one corner of the building a carved pre-Hispanic stone has been used.

Buildings of this type were commonly made with *tezontle*, a porous lava stone of deep maroon color. *Cantera* and *chiluca* stone were often sculpted into baroque decorations to adorn the exterior of these palaces and, invariably, the owner's coat of arms were carved in bas-relief above the door. The carvings around and above the main entrance of this palace are of monsters, animals and flowers. The huge door itself was carved in the Philippines to a Mexican design.

The entrance immediately opens into a spectacular central patio bordered by columns and, on the right side, by a fountain decorated with a two-tailed mermaid playing the guitar and sitting on a head. Unfortunately, the giant yellow tarpaulin which has now been put up over the patio to protect it from the sun bathes the gray stone in an unnatural light which detracts greatly from the effect.

The exhibition rooms are laid out around the patio on the ground and first floors. The museum documents the history of Mexico City from pre-historical times onwards. The first rooms illustrate the geographical topography of the Valley of Mexico, the appearance of man in the valley, the journey of the Aztecs, the founding of Tenochtitlán and the arrival of the Spaniards. Maps and relief models in this section provide a clear exposition of the growth of civilization in this complicated geographical region.

Upstairs a series of rooms provide a historical collage of the city in its various stages of development. Books, furniture, portraits, models of palaces and dressmakers' dummies in period clothes all combine to accentuate important eras of the city's history. Probably the best part of the whole collection is an extensive series of lithographs and engravings of Mexico City in the nineteenth century. These provide a unique view of a city at the height of its glory.

What is not so commonly known is that a further flight of stairs from the second floor of the museum takes one into Joaquin Clausell's studio. Clausell (1866-1935) was undoubtedly one of the greatest Mexican landscape painters of the nineteenth century. The artist's wife was one of the owners of this palace in its later, more rundown years and she used to live in rooms on the first floor. Clausell painted all the walls of his studio not to decorate them but when he had

Stone fountain with mermaid
Mexico City Museum

ideas but no canvasses. They still contain glowing little landscapes, white horses, faces, portraits and heaving seas - all done in a happy, random manner. Not contrived, but simply added to, bit by bit, over the years. Although outside the main scope of the museum, this studio is well worth visiting. It is not well signposted. It is as if there were an upstairs room of a Parisian palace with walls painted and re-painted by a Monet or Van Gogh and no one knew about it!

The museum boasts a magnificent library for the serious student of the city's history and the patio is often used for concerts and other cultural events. It provides an ideal point of departure for anyone who is setting off to explore the treasures of the downtown historical areas of Mexico City. Even Though obviously in need of more funding, foreign visitors regularly rate this museum as number two or three in order of importance.

Museum of Modern Art
Museo de Arte Moderno

Paseo de la Reforma and Gandhi
Bosque de Chapultepec   Map 3

Open: Monday to Sunday 10.00 am to 6.00 pm

When Chapultepec Park was developing its cultural center, the Museum of Modern Art was designed to be one of its showpieces. The low, glass, marble look of the 1960s seems somewhat dated today, and even though this was a purpose-built art museum, its entrance manages to conjure up a hotel lobby more than anything else. The curious moss-green resting place under the stairs suggests more illicit meetings than artistic contemplation - the sort of place where one gets paged when most inappropriate.

Of the four large halls (there are more in the annex behind the main building), two are used for temporary exhibitions which are always well presented and extensively publicized. The museum's permanent collection is in fact a good deal larger than can be accomodated in the space available. Many is the time that references mention the Museum of Modern Art but one can never be sure that the particular work will be on show at the time of one's visit. This is a problem common to museums of this type anywhere in the world.

Hall three (1926-1960) has an impressive welcoming committe of Siqueiros's *Nuestra Imagen Actual;* Orozco's *Paisaje Metafísico* and Tamayo's *Músicos Dormidos.* Further into the hall, the anti-traditional open view arrangement that the gallery opted for takes over. Works of varying levels of intensity can leap into view at almost anytime. Peripheral vision has its disadvantages - like seeing someone else's hand while playing bridge - and the effect can be unsettling for the viewer.

The presence of many foreign artists in this gallery who have been received into the mainstream of Mexican painting is noteworthy, and works by Olga Costa (Germany), Leonora Carrington (England), Alice Rahon (France), Elizabeth Cattlet (U.S.A) and Benito Messegeur (Spain) hang beside the Sorianos, Coronels and Chavezes. Rivera's famous portrait of *Lupe Marín* is also here, and all the paintings are well labeled and have a brief resumé of the artist.

Hall four groups works from the 1970-1980 period which rather implies that a decade has been mislaid somewhere. Turning a blind eye to chronology leaves the other one free to enjoy works by Tamayo, Francisco Corzas, José Luis Cuevas and some enchanting Toledos. He is a self-taught artist from Oaxaca whose genius lies in combining all the authentic symbolism of ancient Mexico with modern techniques. Here as well are Marta Palau's dominating sculptures made from a variety of surprising materials.

In summary, many of the artists in hall three still manage to shock us with their daring ideas and techniques but hall four opens itself to being a trifle too acceptable. Much in the latter is derivative and although there are undoubted patches of excitement, the residual feeling is perhaps of having been let down.

A walk through to the annex (only used for temporary exhibitions) means negotiating a troop of sculptures of different shapes and sizes and in varying media. The appearance is of giant left-over rubbish - as tittilating in its way as debris so often can be. If there is nothing showing in the annex, a browse in the good museum bookshop is preferred before leaving.

National Museum of Musical Instruments

Museo Nacional de Instrumentos Musicales

Liverpool 16, Col. Juárez   Map 5

Open: Monday to Friday 9.30 am to 2.30 pm

One hesitates to classify this as a museum, although there are two rooms of this old house given over to the display of some one hundred and and fifty musical instruments from Mexico and other countries.

The full title of this establishment is the Carlos Chávez National Center of Musical Investigation, Documentation and Information. It is administered jointly by the Secretariat of Education and the National Institute of Bellas Artes.

Of more interest is the extensive library which has been set up here. Serious musicologists should take note of this center which not only advertizes several music-related events which take place in the city, but which also provides an excellent service to researchers.

Museums in the National Palace

Museos en el Palacio Nacional

Palacio Nacional
Plaza de la Constitución, Col. Centro   Map 1

Open: Tuesday to Sunday 10.00 am to 6.00 pm

A visit to the National Palace is on everyone's list when it comes to sightseeing in the city's historic center. Apart from the Diego Rivera murals in the palace which would alone justify the visit, there are two other areas which are catalogued as museums.

Museum in Honor of Benito Juárez
Museo Recinto Homenaje a Benito Juárez

In the North wing of the palace, which is entered by the Puerta Mariana (the one to the left of the main entrance), is this memorial to Benito Juárez. The main room has more the feel of a shrine. To the far end are a bronze bust of Juárez and an open book, also in bronze, which contains the famous letter that Juárez wrote to Mexico's ambassador in Washington in 1865. Down each side, displayed in glass cases, are personal belongings of the great man. To the left as one enters is a substantial library containing historical works, mainly from the Reform period, which can still be used for general reading and research purposes.

Benito Juárez (1806-1872) was unquestionably the most noteworthy Mexican politician and statesman of the mid-nineteenth century. He was a Zapotec Indian from the State of Oaxaca whose schooling was paid for by a Franciscan benefactor. On finishing school, he first entered a seminary in Oaxaca but later changed his vocation and worked his way through law school. He entered local State politics as an alderman in the Oaxaca City Council and gradually worked his way up the political ladder. His first government post was as Secretary of Justice in the Alvarez cabinet of 1855. He was instrumental in drafting the federal Constitution of 1857 which led eventually to the civil war between liberals and conservatives of 1858 to 1861. During this time, it was the Juárez Liberal government, operating from Veracruz, that issued a series of decrees that finally separated church from state in Mexico. In these decrees, births and marriages were made civil ceremonies, all cemeteries were secularized, monastic orders were outlawed and all church properties and assets were nationalized.

Shortly after the Liberals emerged victorious from nearly four years of civil war, the French invasion of 1862 forced Juárez to withdraw his government to San Luís Potosí. He continued in exile during the reign of Emperor Maximilian Von Hapsburg (1864-1867) and returned victorious to Mexico City on July 15, 1867. He was then elected to a third presidential term which was undoubtedly his best. His administration wisely directed its energies into two main fields: a revamping of the economy and a restructuring of the country's educational foundations. Primary education, for instance, was made free and obligatory for the first time. In

1871, Juárez stood for a fourth presidential term and was only narrowly elected. He died from a coronary seizure while still in office on July 19, 1872.

To the right of the shrine area are two rooms which Juárez used when he lived and worked in the National Palace. Here, more than anywhere else in the palace, one has a glimpse of what it must have been like to be a mid-nineteenth century tenant in this, the oldest government residence in the whole of the Americas. All the furnishigs on display, belonged to the Juárez family and were donated to the nation on his death.

Parlamentary Enclosure
Recinto Parlamentario

This part of the palace used to be the Chamber of Deputies until a fire in 1872 forced the Mexican Congress to move to new premises in Donceles street. However, it also contains the room in which the famous Constitution of 1857 was signed and today the area is preserved in recognition of Mexico's parliamentary tradition. A facsimile of the Constitution document is on view as well as plaster reliefs of all the *Constituyentes* (constitutionalists) who were instrumental in the drafting of the document.

Iron chains hang above the facsimile copy of the 1857 Constitution as a reminder of the pledge that this constitution made to free all Mexicans from slavery of whatever sort.

Behind this room is the superbly reconstructed Chamber of Deputies. The space is semi-circular with seats for one hundred and fifty-two deputies facing the two raised presidential chairs - one for the President of the Congress and the other for the President of the Republic. The chamber is rich in symbolism, with the eye of wisdom set into the roof, the red French cap above the raised dias (reminiscent of the influence of the 1791 French Civil Constitution of the Clergy) and the crown which once sat above the image of the Virgin of Guadalupe.

Natural History Museum
Museo de Historia Natural

2a Sección del Nuevo Bosque de Chapultepec   Map 3

Open: Tuesday to Saturday 10.00 am to 5.00 pm
          Sunday 10.00 am to 6.00 pm

In the 1960s Chapultepec Park underwent considerable development with the opening of a number of new museums. The National Museum of Natural History, which opened in 1964, was part of this development and it has since established itself as the second most visited museum in the Metropolitan area.

The four museum modules are clustered together in the shape of domed tents and rather give the impression of a caterpillar crouching in the grass. The interiors have a somewhat unpleasant damp odor about them which one suspects is the result of huge numbers of visitors passing through coupled with poor ventilation. The wear and tear on the museum is plainly visible, although the major showcases are well maintained.

The museum prides itself on being an educational center for both students and the general public, and in a city the size of Mexico it provides a much-needed resource. Walking through the thirteen halls is akin to browsing through a finely illustrated textbook. Starting with the Universe and the planet Earth, subsequent displays deal with the origin of life, taxonomy, the marine world, ecology, evolution, biology, man and bio-geography amongst others. Each section is well-organized and clearly signposted. The space devoted to geological time and evolution is particulary well done with a circular series of models showing the various changes to the Earth's surface and living creatures over millions of years. This is a difficult concept for young people to grasp and here it is handled simply and with considerable imagination.

Tourists might not feel the need to visit this museum as similar ones exist in their own countries. However, for residents (particularly if they have school-age children) a visit here will be immensely rewarding. This is a very busy museum all year round, so one can expect to have stand in line for a few minutes especially on week-ends.

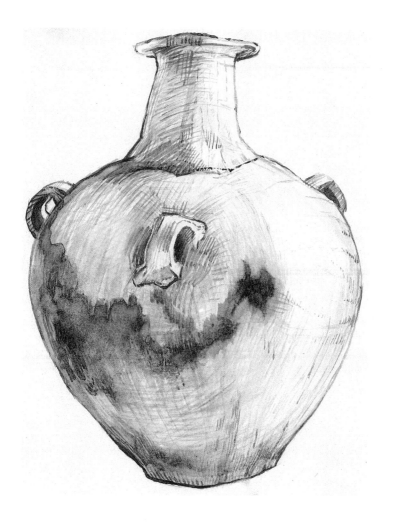

Four-handled clay pot from Michoacán
National Museum of Popular Arts and Industries

National Museum of Popular Arts and Industries

Museo Nacional de Artes e Industrias Populares

Avda. Juárez 44, Col. Centro   Map 1

Open: Tuesday to Sunday 10.00 am to 6.00 pm

The impressive facade of the ex-convent of Corpus Christi stands out from some rather drab surroundings on Avenida Juárez almost opposite the monument to Benito Juárez in the Alameda Park. Built in 1720, an inscription of the same date above the door states that it was the first religious house in the New Spain exclusively for the daughters of high-born Indians. Above this is a carved medallion, topped by a triangular pediment, and a niche with the figure of a saint holding the monstrance.

In 1951 it became a museum under the direction of the National Indigenous Institute and the National Institute of Anthropology and History. Its aim is to promote the varied folk art and industries that abound throughout the Republic of Mexico. Of particular interest is the shop on the same location which has an extensive stock of art and craft items. In fact, the shop is entered via the main entrance while the entrance to the museum proper is through a door found by walking down the right hand side of the building. This is often confusing for the first-time visitor. However, the idea of being able to purchase items similar to those that are on display in the museum area is a good one and well in keeping with the objectives of promoting local arts and crafts.

This simple, low-budget museum displays choice pieces of Mexican folk art, generally dating from the beginnings of this century: wooden masks worn on important feast days; a wide range of pottery produced from the same simple brick kiln design used in pre-Columbian times; hand-blown glass; jewelery and hand-spun or loom-woven textiles of wool, cotton, linen and silk.

After silver, Mexican indigenous dyes were the most important export in early colonial days. Weaving enthusiasts will enjoy the cases showing the age-old processes of dye-making in Mexico. Some of the indigenous dyes include the cochineal dye which comes from an insect picked off plants by hand and then boiled and pounded on a *metate.* The purpura dye (the color of popes and kings) is extracted from a shellfish that lives on rocks on the Mexican Pacific coast. The beige and yellow colors come from dyes processed from lichens and barks.

Folk art is born from the talent of making the most of what the country around will yield up, however poor. The small jewelry section has some haunting examples of this creative process in the fragile string of tiny, dried-yellow flowers and a necklace of Venetian trade beads interspersed with with pomegranate seeds. The latter is also a good example of the amazing adaptability of folk art to new cultures and objects, which are then slowly absorbed only to emerge, often centuries later, in subtly changed forms.

This is a rich area for the arts and crafts shopper for, apart from this museum and shop, there are also two branches of the government-sponsored FONART stores close by to the left up Avenida Juárez as you leave this museum.

National Museum of Popular Cultures
Museo Nacional de Culturas Populares

Hidalgo 289, Coyoacán   Map 4

Open: Tuesday to Saturday 10.00 am to 8.00 pm
        (closes 4.00 pm Tuesdays and Thursdays)
        Sunday 11:00 am to 5:00 pm

The origin of this museum goes back to the late 1970s when a group of anthropologists began to question the traditional role of museums within the context of Mexican popular cultures. They defined the need for a more dynamic museum which would, in conjunction with both urban and rural community groups, mount a series of thematic exhibitions related to popular culture. Once these shows (many of them appear as popular festivals) had been assembled, they would be opened to the public for periods of six months or even longer. Then, in tune with this idea, each exhibition would be returned to the community that had produced it in the first place. The circle would be completed by donating the entire exhibition to some museum in the provinces instead of putting it into cold storage.

The guiding principle which motivates the Museum of Popular Cultures works well in a country which is as culturally rich as Mexico. Possibly more than any other country, Mexico has a very diverse number of popular groups each with its own characteristic brand of creativity. Rather than rigidify these expressions of popular culture, the museum attempts to involve communities in celebrations of their own work and thus promote its further expression and development.

A good example of this was one of the museum's first major exhibitions entitled, *Corn: The Basis of Popular Mexican Culture.* Another, called *The Circus*, was the result of successful collaboration between museum staff and the circus community in Mexico. In addition to the temporary exhibitions, the Museum of Popular Cultures runs parallel competitions, round-table discussions, food festivals and activities for children, all of which emphasize the vitality of the institution itself.

Visitors will therefore be taking pot luck if they visit the museum on the off chance, but details of current offerings are well advertised in the local press.

Postal Museum
Museo Postal

Central Post Office
Av. Lázaro Cárdenas and Tacuba, Col. Centro   Map 1

Open: Monday to Friday 8.00 am to 3.00 pm
        Saturday 9.00 am to 1.00 pm

This sumptious building just across from Bellas Artes (see entry) is one of the famous landmarks of the downtown area of Mexico City. The Italian architect, Adamo Boari, who also designed the Bellas Artes Palace, was entrusted with this project in 1902. The style is heavily Italian renaissance and, as such, it remains as a fine illustration of the cultural mood of the Porfiriato (late nineteenth and early twentieth century) when Mexico showed a marked preference for all things European.

It was purpose built as the general administrative building for the Mexican postal service and was inaugurated as such by Porfirio Díaz in 1907. With such glorious headquarters, it might be supposed that the Mexican Post Office would offer a service to match. However, even the most generous of assessments would have to admit that the Mexican mail has rarely progressed beyond the lackluster during the last eighty years.

On the second floor there is a small museum and library devoted to the history and development of the postal service in Mexico. Philatelists should not expect to see rare collections of stamps, although the museum does have a complete collection of Mexican issues.

National Museum of Printing
Museo Nacional de la Estampa

Av. Hidalgo 39, Col. Centro   Map 1

Open: Tuesday to Sunday 10.00 am to 6.00 pm

This is almost next door to the Franz Mayer Museum (see entry) and to two of the city's colonial churches, La Santa Veracruz and San Juan de Díos, in an attractive little square a few yards up Avenida Hidalgo from Bellas Artes (see entry).

The museum itself is in a pink-colored colonial house which has been extensively restored. Enter through large wood doors into a light-filled patio. Above is an oval, railed gallery under the stained glass dome. All the downstairs rooms are used for temporary exhibitions and only two rooms on the second floor contain the museum's permanent displays.

Room one contains the tools used in various forms of etchings and wood and lino cuts. They are displayed in cases with half-finished work or finished plates with the results on paper. The emphasis in the permanent sections is on technique and provides a helpful background to appreciating the other work on show. In room two a fine antique lithographic press stands in the center. Other display cases show the process involved in woodcuts and the different methods used in engraving.

Of particular note in the permanent collection are some original works by José Guadalupe Posada (1851-1913). Posada was a printmaker who had a great influence on modern Mexican art. His famous zinc etching, *Calavera Catrina*, can be seen here. These skeleton motifs are still used in Mexico today for decorating cakes and chocolate skulls for the Day of the Dead celebrations (November 1 and 2). Posada's output was monumental and when he died in 1913 he left a fertile legacy of several thousand popular engravings and etchings which are still influential today.

One of the museum's objectives is to foster an interest in the graphic arts amongst the public in general and young people in particular. For this purpose the museum shows two video programs on woodcuts, etching, lithography, dry point and other graphic techniques. The first program runs sixty-one minutes and the second, forty-five. To be able to see the graphic masters at work is extremely motivating to anyone seriously interested in this art form. For many of us, the whole process of *estampa* can be even more exciting than the results (the word has a much wider meaning in Spanish than the translation of 'printing' conveys).

Museum of Remembrance
Museo de Recuerdo

Donceles 66, Col. Centro   Map 6

Open: By appointment only
    ☎ 510-2267 & 521-5571

The Spanish and French Academies are famed (and often feared) institutions. The Mexican Academy, founded in 1875, is no exception. In 1970, members of the Academy decided to open a museum to both further the work of the Academy itself and also to provide a monument of remembrance to all its past members.

The house itself is an attractive *tezontle* stone building of two storeys which was once a private home. Carved wooden doors open into a square central patio. The two small galleries off the patio contain original manuscripts and other literary memorabilia of Mexico's finest poets and writers from about 1875 onwards. Upstairs there is an extensive library containing the best of Mexican literature and Spanish translations of other works. Much of the library was donated by ex-President López Mateos.

Visitors to the museum can see literary fragments (often inspired notes on rough paper), letters, photographs, portraits of the men of letters and the medals and prizes which are the public recognition of things of written beauty. Things in fact, which are all too easily lost or discarded unless there is a concerted effort to record them for posterity. Writing (or any artistic endeavor) is a lonely business, and one can understand the basic urge behind the formation of groups whether they be in academy conference rooms or Parisian cafés. Unfortunately, however, those who inherit or even donate these touching and evocative fragments often find it hard to share them with the general public. This museum, in line with this tendency, can only be visited by appointment which seems a pity especially when one considers the breadth and depth of the library alone. Researchers, and other interested parties should surely be encouraged to make use of these fine facilities. Is not remembrance to do in part with re-enactment?

Mexican writers and their works that we are invited to

remember in this museum include: Francisco Monterde, Rubén Darío, Carlos Pellicer, Salvador Novo, Antonio Médiz Bolio, Alfonso Reyes, José Vasconcelos and Federico Gamboa amongst others. The list begs the question of where were all the women writers and what have they been doing since 1875?

We suspect that, aside from its undoubted intellectual and elitist appeal, the Mexican Academy and its parallel museum needs much more definition as to the role it wishes to play in the country's literary and cultural life.

National Museum of The Revolution
Museo Nacional de la Revolución

Monumento a la Revolución
Plaza de la República, Col. San Rafael   Map 5

Open: Tuesday to Sunday 9.00 am to 5.00 pm

The best view of this solid, heavy monument to the Revolution is from Avenida Juárez driving up from the Alameda. The museum is located in the monument's basement. Originally, under Porfirio Díaz's government, the structure was going to be a new Legislative Palace. With the outbreak of the Revolution, all work ceased and it was not until 1933 that it continued. This time, architect Obregón Santacilia converted it into a monument to the Revolution, and in each of the four supporting columns, are the remains of five of the most revered revolutionaries: Madero, Carranza, Calles, Villa and Cárdenas.

The exhibition provides a chronological narrative of the Mexican Revolution in all its social, economic and political aspects from the end of the Porfiriato to the proclamation of the 1917 Constitution. The space has been divided into five discrete sections which document the identifiable phases of the first major revolution in the twentieth century. The use of photos, realia, maps, newspaper cuttings, newsreel footage, and life-size models and reconstructions have all been cleverly orchestrated to achieve some imaginative effects. The creative use of audiovisual elements involves the visitor from the start and one's attention is rarely left to wander. One such example is the figure of Madero campaigning which has been blown up from a newspaper cutting, mounted in 3-D and presented with an accompanying soundtrack of one of his political rallies. By such innovative use of display techniques, the essence of the moment is nicely captured.

When armed outbreaks initiated the Mexican Revolution in 1910, their prime objective was the ousting of Porfirio Díaz who had ruled the country uninterruptedly since 1876. However, what began as a relatively straightforward political movement, soon began to broaden into a major economic and social upheaval which was to engulf the whole country in a bloody civil war. During the long revolutionary struggle in its military phase (1913-1917), the Mexican people developed a sense of identity and purpose in a way that other Latin American peoples have been unable to match. The climax to the Revolution was reached in 1917 when a new Constitution was promulgated. While this did not pacify all revolutionary groups, the new Constitution at least set the goals towards which successive presidents were to work.

One of the rooms visited at the end of the chronological display is devoted to a photographic reconstruction (with three dimensional elements) of the effects of the multiple civil wars on Mexico City. The whole montage manages to fascinate and move, and deserves the highest praise as an artistic display.

The Mexican Revolution stands out by far as the most momentous period in the nation's recent history. It is satisfying to think that this museum lives up to that same level of importance.

Emiliano Zapata

Risco House Museum
Museo de la Casa del Risco

Plaza San Jacinto 15, Col. San Angel Inn   Map 2

Open: Tuesday to Friday 10.00 am to 3.00 pm.
       Saturday and Sunday 10.00 am to 2.00 pm.

Two houses down from the famous Bazar Sábado in San Angel is this little jewel of an eighteenth century country house which opened as a public museum in 1962.

Called *Risco* because of its quite outstanding baroque porcelain fountain in the main patio (*risco* meaning porcelain or stoneware), this huge folly is made of Chinese porcelain, mother-of-pearl, talavera from Puebla and some Japanese and English porcelain. The fountain itself is a not-so-little jewel which dominates the central patio.

Don Isidro Fabela, who donated the Casa del Risco to the nation, had it restored between 1933 and 1953. He was a serious art collector who, in his own words, "spent what money I had in the auction houses of London, Paris, The Hague and Madrid." Little by little he built up a reasonably sized collection. Don Isidro again: "I have no pretensions that it contains works of the greatest painters. The works I have, I bought because I liked them, and because I wanted them for the pleasure of my eyes and the solace of my spirit. . . to share with our people and others."

Don Isidro was an intellectual and, aside from his artistic pursuits, he was a one-time Mexican ambassador and a governor of the State of Mexico. His bequest to the nation, the Casa del Risco, has had a chequered past: a family home, a garrison for the U.S. army in 1847 and, so the legend goes, a lodging for Zapata and his revolutionary cohorts.

A good collection of Don Isidro's paintings (mainly European, but with some Mexican colonial) are on view on the ground floor of the Casa de Risco. On the upper floor are a series of rooms which he furnished with antique pieces in a style typical of a Mexican country house of the period. This museum is well worth a short visit, and can be fitted in either before or after a shopping spree in the Bazar Sábado just up the road.

Rufino Tamayo Museum
Museo Rufino Tamayo

Paseo de la Reforma and Gandhi
Col. Bosque de Chapultepec   Map 3

Open: Tuesday to Sunday 10.00 am to 6.00 pm

This purpose-built museum was created to house an important collection of modern art donated to the nation by Rufino Tamayo and his wife Olga. The multi-leveled structure made of rough concrete, wood and glass, cleverly mingles natural and artificial light in varied interior areas to produce a diversity of atmospheres and space. Construction began in 1979 and the museum, initially administered by the communications conglomerate Televisa, opened to the public in 1981.

Of the ten galleries, six contain permanent exhibits of Tamayo's work as well as a marvellously representative collection of major international modern artists. The latter have the added interest of reflecting Tamayo's taste, and they make up an impressive shopping list of great modern painters. They are all fine examples of each artist. Among these are works by Magritte, Salvador Dali, Max Ernst, Graham Sutherland, Willen de Kooning, Andy Warhol and Roy Lichenstein.

The galleries provoke a feeling of spaciousness and calm, helped by very high ceilings, although it is not always easy to work out the route one should follow through them. A sloping ramp from the first gallery leads to Tamayo's own works. These are displayed in chronological order and show the artist's development from his early restricted palette and formal academic style (though always with a hint of something else, usually Cubism) to his ethereal *Mujer en Blanco* (1976). By the fifties shape and texture are predominant and he has left formal composition behind. There seems to be no color that he cannot experiment with. A fine example of one of his famous *Sandías* (watermelons) runs through the luscious gamut of reds and crimsons. His wife Olga features in four paintings dating from 1934 to his *Retrato Conyugal* painted in 1981.

Tamayo was born in 1899 in Oaxaca of Zapotec Indian

ancestry. Orphaned at the age of twelve, he came to Mexico City to live with an aunt. There he entered the Academy of San Carlos but soon left to study independently. In 1921 he became Head of the Department of Ethnographic Drawing at the National Museum of Archeology and became fascinated with pre-Columbian art. Tamayo reacted against the rhetoric and epic proportions of the Mexican mural movement and preferred to work on a smaller scale using Cubist, Surrealist and other European styles, which he fused with Mexican subject matter. By the thirties he had become a well-known Mexican painter and in 1950 when his work achieved such a success at the Venice Biennale, he achieved international recognition. Although he has painted several murals in Mexico City and elsewhere, his oil paintings are usually considered to be his liveliest vehicle of expression.

The Rufino Tamayo is equipped with an auditorium to seat nearly two hundred people and a varied program of plays, concerts, dances and other cultural activities are offered every year. This is undoubtedly a first-class museum and it is difficult to walk away without being dazzled by the quality of work on show.

San Carlos Museum
Museo de San Carlos

Puente de Alvarado 50, Col. Tabacalera   Map 1

Open: Monday to Sunday 10.00 am to 6.00 pm.
          Closed Tuesdays and Public Holidays.

Both the building and the art gallery that it now houses have fascinating histories. The former was originally the old Palace of the Count of Buenavista, built by Manuel Tolsá in the early nineteenth century. It is basically neoclassical with a few tinges of baroque. The famous oval patio is said to have been inspired by the great round patio in Charles V's palace in the Alhambra, Granada. The light gray *cantera* quarry stone of the columns and imposing staircase provide just the right touch of grandeur with which to offset this fine collection of paintings. In quality and quantity the whole is well balanced.

The origins of this collection (mainly Mexican and international paintings with some sculptures and engravings) date back to the ancient Royal Academy of San Carlos which was founded in 1785 by Viceroy Matías de Gálvez. It was Gerónimo Antonio Gil, chief engraver of the Royal Mint, who arrived in Mexico in 1778 and conceived the idea of founding an art school, which soon became a museum thanks to the works left behind by graduating students and donations from various sources. In certain centuries there was never a more effective way of boosting an art collection than by closing the odd monastery or convent. The Royal Academy profited from a bout of such closures in 1782 (the Jesuits) and again in 1855 when Antonio López de Santa Anna invited the remaining Mexican religious houses to donate their best pictures to the Academy.

Back to the palace itself. Unfortunately, the Count of Buenavista never lived long enough to enjoy the palace which was to have been a present from his loving mother, María Josefa de Pinillo y Gómez. Piqued perhaps by the untimely demise of her son, she sold the palace and, for over a century, it continued to change hands with remarkable rapidity. A few other counts, the odd prince, a past head of state (Santa Anna) and a couple of military gentlemen saw out the nineteenth century.

Since 1900, the owners or tenants have been somewhat less illustrious: the Tabacalera Mexicana Tobacco Company (until 1933), the National Lottery (1933-1946), the Secretariat of Comunications and Public Works and a public high school. The checquered ownership saga came to a timely end in 1968 when it was officially inaugurated as the museum it is today.

This large collection cuts a fairly impressive path through five centuries of art: from early fourteenth century religious painting up to the nineteenth century. High points along the way include works by Lucas Cranach 'El Viejo', both Tintorretos (father and son), some works by Zubarán and Rubens, portraits attributed to Sir Joshua Reynolds, a Brueghal, a genuine Goya (they also have a copy), a *John the Baptist* by Ingres and an important collection of works by Landesio, a notable artist and a past Director of the Royal Academy of San Carlos.

The San Carlos Museum is highly recommended. This

international collection of paintings is one of the most important in the country displayed in a setting of rare architectural beauty.

Viceroy Art Gallery of San Diego
Pinacoteca Virreinal de San Diego

Dr. Mora 7, Col. Centro

Map 1

Open: Tuesday to Sunday 9.00 am to 5.00 pm

This museum is housed in the ex-monastery of San Diego which dates from 1591. The first monks were members of the reformed, barefoot, Franciscan order whose rule of austerity forbade them owning property of any kind. The monastery buildings and church had been donated to the monks by Don Mateo de Mauleón, but as they rejected property ownership as such, a curious ceremony took place every year on Good Friday. Once the Good Friday liturgy had taken place, the entire community abandoned the church and buildings and the abbot, who was the last to leave, ceremoniously locked the doors and handed over the keys of the buildings to their rightful, legal owners. The latter, after another ceremonial pause, returned the keys to the abbot once more, and in so doing, acquiesed in granting the community another year's tenure of the monastery.

The art collection now hangs in what was the main nave and side chapel of the church. There are some two hundred and fifty paintings from the sixteenth, seventeenth and eighteenth centuries - the three hundred year period of viceregal government of Mexico by Spain. Most of the works originally belonged to monasteries and convents established in the New Spain. A large part of the collection was saved by Bernardo Couto and added to the Academy of San Carlos (see entry) until this present museum was officially established in 1964.

During the viceregal period, the visual arts were used to teach the indigenous people a new religion and a new culture. As Indian masons learned to build churches and carve stone angels and saints, so the artists learned to paint Biblical scenes in oil paint on canvas, wood or metal bases (usually copper or zinc). Outstanding artists of this period in Mexican art - Luis and José Juárez, Sebastian López de Arteaga, Simón Pereyns, the three Echaves, Luis Legarto and Miguel Cabrera - are all well represented in this unique collection.

The high ceilings provide an ideal hanging space for these very large paintings. In general, the paintings are in good condition and the antique frames alone are well worth admiring. However, the overall impression might overwhelm the modern day visitor given the profusion of religious themes and almost alien scenes that are depicted. Curiously, one is struck by the preponderance of children, cherubs and scattered flowers that appear in so many of these paintings, far more so than would be the case in their European counterparts. This is perhaps an instance of indigenous Mexican painters still preserving their ancient cultural values in the face of the new religion. Children and flowers were both highly prized in pre-Hispanic Mexican cultures.

Apart from the religious paintings, this collection does have some fine landscapes and still lifes which merit careful study. The museum also arranges an excellent series of musical and other parallel cultural events, and its monthly bulletin of events, available from the museum, is a useful publication.

Santo Domingo Cultural Center (Juan Cordero Room)
Centro Cultural Santo Domingo (Sala Juan Cordero)

Brasil 37 esq. Colombia, Col. Centro   Map 6

Open: Tuesday to Saturday 10.00 am to 6.00 pm
      Sunday 10.00 am to 5.00 pm

Until recently this colonial house was known as the Juan Cordero Room after the Mexican painter of that name (1824-1884). In fact the house, which dates from the late sixteenth century and which was once used as lodgings for members of the Holy Inquisition, passed into the Cordero family through marriage and belonged not to the painter Juan, but to his brother Manuel.

It has been extensively restored and is a fine example of a moderately large colonial home. It is roomy without being ostentatious and very evocative of the 'old Mexico'. High wooden doors lead to a square, flagstoned patio open to the sky. To the far end of the patio wide stone and *talavera* stairs lead to the second floor. Here the original wooden balustrade is amazingly still in place (so many of them were destroyed and used as fire wood). The earthenware pots with flowers and hanging plants create the atmosphere of a family residence rather than a museum.

The idea behind the Santo Domingo Cultural Center is to arrange temporary exhibits and to show period furniture on the upper floor. Much of the latter used to belong to the Cordero family and is being gradually taken out of storage. A small number of Juan Cordero's paintings may also be transferred here.

The upstairs rooms are of perfect proportions, all looking over the central patio. From here one can enjoy an almost theatrically beautiful skyscape of towers and belfries. For anyone interested in museum-homes, a visit here will be highly recommended. This center is yet another extremely positive testimony to the excellent work of restoration which has been gathering pace over the last few years in the historic center of Mexico City.

Siqueiros Public Art Gallery
Sala de Arte Público Siqueiros

Tres Picos 29, Col. Polanco   Map 3

Open: Monday to Friday 10.00 am to 5.00 pm
          Saturday 10.00 am to 1.00 pm

It is only right and fitting that internationally-renowned muralists such as David Alfaro Siqueiros should live up to the
larger-than-life dimensions of their paintings. From his birth
in Chihuahua in 1896 to his death in 1973, Siqueiros proved
that he was not the diminutive, retiring sort. By the age of elev-
en, he had already copied a Raphael Madonna, and by fifteen he was enrolled in the Academy of Fine Arts in Mexico
City and was leading a student strike. His experiences as a
political activist, soldier, executive committee member of the
Mexican Communist party and prisoner are as grand scale
as his fifty or so major murals.

In 1914 he fought with Venustiano Carranza's Constitutionalist army in the Mexican Revolution, and in 1937 he was
again in action on the loyalist side in the Spanish Civil War. In
between he had met Diego Rivera in Paris (1925), with whom
he discussed radical theoretical guidelines for 'a new social
art', and had already spent several periods in jail. For several
years (1925-1930), he gave up painting to devote himself
exclusively to revolutionary union activities. His prodigious
output extended to books, articles, pamphlets and innumera-
ble lecture tours throughout the world. He aroused considerable hatred and jealousy as well as widespread curiosity
and devotion. He was not surprisingly fêted behind the iron
curtain, and in 1967, received the Lenin Peace Prize from the
Soviet Union, the money from which he donated to the people of North Vietnam.

In his last years he completed the monumental Siqueiros Cultural Polyforum on Insurgentes Avenue. While at
times, his life reads not unlike a Graham Greene novel, one
cannot help but warm to the politically-motivated artist who
found time to publish a book so prosaically entitled, *How to
Paint a Mural* (1951).

The Siqueiros Public Art Gallery was his house and
workshop in Mexico City which he bequeathed to the nation

as a last wish. Nothing domestic remains of the interior which has been completely gutted to house large scale photographs and mock-ups of several of his murals. A large part of the ground floor is given over to his mural, *Maternidad* which he started in 1971 and which was to have hung in a school in the State of Mexico. On the upper floors are some well-documented sketches and doodles for major mural works. Somehow one's fascination for mural painting is increased when one sees these roughs, so minute in comparison to the final execution.

Out of perhaps a dozen of his smaller canvasses on display, *Cristo de Pueblo* (1963) and *Retrato de Angelica Arenal de Siqueiros* (1947) alone justify a visit here. When confronted with these two works, both outside his mainstream socially conscious muralism, one is left wondering if there were not still aspects of his talent that might have emerged if only his life had been quieter and less turbulent.

Cloister of Sor Juana Inés de la Cruz
Museo del Claustro de Sor Inés de la Cruz

San Jerónimo 47, Col. Centro   Map 1

Open: Monday to Friday 9.00 am to 6.00 pm

Sor Juana Inés de la Cruz (1648 - 1695) undoubtedly claims a place as one of Mexico's most famous women of letters. In a period when few women ever aspired to more than a rudimentary education, Sor Juana Inés was largely self-taught. She grew from a child prodigy who amazed intellectuals at the viceregal court into a beautiful, graceful young woman with astonishing talents. An early champion of women's rights, she wrote in one of her poems:

> *Hombres necios que acusáis*
> *a la mujer sin razón,*
> *sin ver que sois la ocasión*
> *de lo mismo que culpáis;* (1)

At the age of nineteen she stunned her admirers by passing up favorable prospects of marriage and taking the veil as a nun in the order of Discalced Carmelites. She transfered her vocation a short time later to the less rigorous order of Conceptionist nuns who had founded the San Jerónimo Convent in 1585. Here, in this monastery, Sor Juana Inés, the nun-poetess, wrote all her works - mainly prose and lyric poetry, including some passionate, almost erotic love poetry of great beauty. Although always constant in her faith, she never aspired to being a spiritual mystic. Hers was a far more rational and intellectual mind that had been widely admired and quoted in court circles. At an early age, and because of her reputation as a somewhat precocious young intellect, Sor Juana Inés had been invited to meet the viceroy and his wife, the latter becoming her most ardent patron. Always prey to great anxiety which increasingly sapped her strength, Sor Juana Inés de la Cruz eventually succumbed to an attack of the plague which ravaged the city and which took her life on April 17, 1695.

The San Jerónimo convent in which she had lived most of her adult life was finally closed by government order in 1857. From that date, the buildings fell into both disuse and abuse of various kinds. A little over a hundred years later, in the late 1960s, hardly anything of the once famous convent remained; and if had not had been for the intervention of Sra. Margarita López Portillo in 1971, perhaps it would have been lost forever. Since then, extensive restoration efforts have been undertaken to salvage what little remains of the San Jerónimo convent. Today, the vast central patio and cloisters are open to the public. During recent excavations, the remains of some nuns' cells and other convent installations have come to light. It is now apparent that each cell had its own talavera-tiled bathroom en suite. However, those who expect to see a replica of Sor Juana Inés de la Cruz's cell or a collection of her books will be disappointed. They are not here. The original cells, when she entered the convent, were more like *casitas* rather in the style of hotel bungalows with all services. She would, for instance, probably have retained the services of her own cook and had a private dining room in which to entertain guests. In Sor Juana's time, because of her preeminent position in the world of letters, the convent had become a very prestigious center of culture and literature. Over one hundred of her poems were written in honor of musicians, writers, courtiers and other well known notables

Sor Juana Inés de la Cruz

who became, in turn, followers of this most erudite of nuns in the New Spain. When her first volume of poems, *Inundación Castálida*, was published in Madrid, Sor Juana became known as the 'Tenth Muse'. Visiting the site today, one is left with the feeling more of exacavated ancient ruins than with the relics of seventeenth century religious life. Archeological fragments that were unearthed during restoration have been left as sad reminders of a golden age of religious architecture and institutions in Mexico City. The collections amount to little more than potsherds rather than objects: a little piece of blue porcelain here, a crystal wine glass there, but whether they once adorned Sor Juana's dinner table or belonged to some other, later age, is not told. In the square in front of the church is a statue of the famous poetess. Sor Juana Inés de la Cruz would surely have approved of the present day uses to which her convent site has been put. Today, the Claustro de Sor Juana Institution is a non-profit organization that organizes and sponsors a wide range of cultural and educational activities.

(¹) Ah stubborn men, unreasonable
In blaming woman's nature,
Oblivious that your acts incite
The very faults you censure.

Translated by Robert Graves. *Chicano Literature: Text and Context* (Englewood Cliffs, N.J., 1972), pp. 10-11. The word 'stubborn' for *necios* is preferred by the present authors over Graves' text which indicates 'stupid'.

Museum of Technology
Museo Tecnológico

Bosque de Chapultepec 2a. Sección   Map 3

Open: Tuesday to Saturday 9.00 am to 5.00 pm
       Sunday 9.00 am to 1.00 pm

This museum was founded in 1970 by the Federal Commission of Electricity. Its main raison d'être is to promote an awareness of and interest in the sciences and technology among young people. It is an outstandingly good example of what the authorities in Mexico are doing to make their museums live places of learning for young people. Mexico is a country where sixty-five percent of its population are still under fifteen years of age, and the need to train and motivate this youthful population in the sciences and technology is a very pressing one.

There are several indoor thematic exhibition halls dedicated to electricity, transport, physics, astronomy and a whole pavillion given over to the oil industry as well as some outdoor exhibits in the museum's gardens. A great deal of the material on display is three dimensional and in working order. In fact, one of the great strengths of this museum is its insistance on a hands-on interaction between the objects displayed and the visitor. To back this up, the museum staff also provide a series of short courses and programs for school children and others which are instructional and motivational in the areas of science and technology.

The Museum of Technology caters for a wide ability range from primary and secondary school right up to the university and professional levels. However, the main impetus is geared towards to younger age range who, says Director González de la Mora, "are the new public who are coming into contact with science for the first time." In the transport section there are several old locomotives on display, and in one of the railway carriages, there is a young person's library staffed by trained professionals in which children can consult a good selection of educational materials.

Large parties of school childern regularly visit the Museum of Technology and it is also highly recommended for family visits. The facilities are extensive (a library, auditorium and bookshop are all available on the site) and the museum deserves to be applauded for the contribution it makes to extending the science and technology school curricula of the classroom to the practical everyday world outside.

Templo Mayor Museum
Museo del Templo Mayor

Facing Argentina Street
Behind Cathedral, Col. Centro   Map 1

Open: Tuesday to Sunday 9.00 am to 5.00 pm

February 21, 1978 will undoubtedly prove to be one of the most significant dates in the history of Mexico City. Near daybreak on that day, some workmen who were digging ditches for an electric cable at the corner of Guatemala and Argentina streets hit something hard. They could see that the object that had interrupted their work was a stone decorated in relief. All work stopped, and the find was reported. Just two days later, an excavation began that uncovered an extraordinary monument: a circular carved stone illustrating the dismembered body of Coyolxauhqui (*koh-yohl-shau-kee*), sister of Huitzilopochtli (*Wee-shi-lo-pos-tli*), the Aztec god of war. The workmen had uncovered significant remains of the Great Temple or *Templo Mayor* of Tenochtitlán, the capital city of the Aztec Empire. This important archeological discovery acted as a catalyst on a project that had been planned some time before: the complete excavation of the Great Temple.

A little background: The Aztecs were the last nomadic tribe to enter the Valley of Mexico, and they were beginning to acquire some notoriety about two hundred years before the Spanish conquest. By about 1345 the Aztecs had eventually settled on the marshy edges of the great lake. Having occupied a small island, they acquired, through trade, sufficient materials with which to enlarge their foothold. From very insignificant beginnings they gradually succeeded in creating the great city of Tenochtitlán.

From their first appearance in the valley, the Aztecs were grudgingly admired by rulers of the other city states. They were a young, vigorous people, hungry and ambitious. They were also superb warriors, and it was as mercenaries, exploiting the tenuous balance of power in Anáhuac (the name of the great valley) that they first achieved recognition. Prior to

121

moving to their island redoubt, they had occupied Chapulte-pec hill. When they began to construct Tenochtitlán, they connected the city to the mainland via a number of cause-ways - one of which was to Chapultepec, their main source of drinking water. It was an inspired defensive concept.

One of their first building endeavors was the construc-tion of a temple in honor of their gods. This was to be the center not only of their city, but also of their world. Their power and prestige, and with these their empire, grew rap-idly. By the beginning of the sixteenth century their sphere of influence covered most of central and much of Southern Mexico. By the time Moctezuma came to power in 1502, the island capital of Tenochtitlán was a most impressive city. How large it was in terms of population is difficult to tell. However, even conservative estimates which put the popula-tion at around eighty thousand inhabitants would have made Tenochtitlán one of the largest cities in the world at that time. Only four European cities at that time (Paris, Venice, Milan and Naples) had populations in excess of one hundred thou-sand. The amazement of the Spanish conquerors at their first sight of Tenochtitlán is therefore quite understandable. Cor-tés wrote of, "the magnificence, the strange and marvellous things of this great city," which itself was "so remarkable as not to be believed." The central part of the city (roughly where the present day Zócalo is) must have swarmed with activity. Thousands of people gathered to barter and gossip in the market places. In the center of it all was the great tem-ple with its double pyramids dedicated to Huitzilopochtli and Tláloc. Around the temple, those first Spaniards would have seen great royal palaces and other enormous civic struc-tures.

Today, as one approaches the Great Temple and its museum adjunct, some of that market atmosphere of Tenochtitlán still reaches over the centuries. Around the site street vendors still ply their trade. On the sidewalks, the women still set out their rush mats piled high with fruit and vegetables while noises from a political rally waft across from the Zócalo.

The Great Temple: When the Spaniards entered Tenochti-tlán and saw the great Aztec temple for the first time, they little realized that what they were gazing at in awe was little more than a shell. The stone and mortar walls that formed the outer construction of the temple covered at least four other

Figurine and objects from Monte Alban, Oaxaca
National Museum of Anthropology

complete structures. These structures, stacked like nested boxes one on top of each other, were the results of successive Aztec rulers both repairing previous structures and enlarging the temple for the purposes of aggrandizement or rededication. The earliest temple probably dates from around 1350 A.D. It is now known, however, that the original temple was enlarged at least seven times on all sides. This process is fully explained by the fact that the buildings of Tenochtitlán continually suffered from fractures due to earth movements and subsidence. In addition, several Aztec rulers between the late fourteenth and early sixteenth centuries ordered the rebuilding and enlarging of the temple. It was at such times that, to pay homage to the gods, a great quantity of jewels and precious stones were deposited in the new layers of rubble which were to form the foundations of the new temple facades. This fact was corroborated by one of the early Spanish chroniclers, Bernal Díaz del Castillo, who recalled that when the Spaniards began to dig the foundations for a new church on the site of the temple that they had destroyed, "they found much gold, silver, chalchuite, pearls, crude pearls and other stones."

What the conquerors had seen when they first entered Tenochtitlán was a huge temple, facing west, rising to a height of about sixty meters with a dual staircase climbing to double shrines: Huitzilopochtli's shrine to the right and Tláloc's to the left. In front of each of these were round stones or blocks on which victims would have been sacrificed to appease the gods.

The Excavation Project: In 1790 and again at various times in the present century, there had been archeological finds and minor excavations on the temple site. However, the find in 1978 precipitated the first major, comprehensive excavation project. The project was organized in three phases. The first phase consisted of consolidating all the information available about the Great Temple from both archeological and historical sources. From this well of knowledge, certain hypotheses were adopted with which to guide the excavation project itself. It was, for example, hypothesised that the presence of shrines dedicated to Tlaloc (god of water and rain) and Huitzilopochtli (god of war) on top of the temple was testimony to the fundamental needs of the Mexica people. Their economy was based on the twin pillars of agriculture and military conquest of surrounding tribes who then had to pay tributes to the Mexica. If this original hypothesis was proved to be correct, then all the elements associated with the temple would in some way be suggestive of the fundamental necessities of the people who built it. Historical sources, in the form of writings of the early chroniclers, had mentioned the presence of the gods of Tláloc and Huitzilopochtli on the temple heights.

The second phase of the project was the physical excavation itself. Here great care had to be taken to assess the effect this would have on the streets, drains and buildings in the urban center. The excavations started in earnest on March 20, 1978 beginning at the bases of the three temple facades facing the north, south and east. A parking lot and a city street covered most of the area so few existing structures were demolished. As the project developed, some other structures had to be removed but none of great historical significance. During this phase, it became obvious that the final layer of the temple's construction had been razed to the foundations. The temple had of course been destroyed at the conquest and many of its stones used for the construction of early colonial buildings. However, the older layers of the temple, which was made up of one construction on top of another, were found to be in better conditions. Another limiting factor in this excavation phase was the natural water level of the city center. This is to be found approximately five meters below the present day street level and it naturally prevented deeper excavations of some of the earlier levels of the temple.

The third phase of the project was the interpretation phase. During the excavations (1978-1982), some seven thousand archeological artefacts were collected. These were unearthed in stone-walled chests, the remains of stone household boxes, and in the fill-in or stone and mud rubble layer that had been used to cover an earlier temple structure. The location and positioning of these artefacts clearly had a purpose and a symbolism, the understanding of which still needs research. In general, the initial hypothesis proved correct for most of the material that was found is related either to Tláloc or Huitzilpochtli.

The Templo Mayor Museum: As with the National Museum of Anthropology (see entry), the first time visitor to the Templo Mayor Museum must be prepared for an onslaught of information. The story of the Aztecs, how they came to settle in the valley of Mexico, the building of Tenochtitlán and the history of the Great Temple itself is fatiguing for the novice. The borders between history and legend, and between fact and fiction, are never clearly drawn. However, this museum does a splendid job in relating a complicated story well.

Inside, the museum is cool and more muted in contrast to the world outside. On each of the four floors a large smoked-glass window affords a good view over the temple site and the skyscape of crooked basilicas and the slanting perspectives of colonial houses in disrepair. Seemingly, the cultures continue to clash.

The many treasures contained here are exquisitely displayed. Objects are exhibited according to an open plan. They are not all pushed against the wall, and visitors can benefit from walking round them. Good taste and imagination are everywhere in evidence. The glass display cases contain a rich variety of objects culled over a long period of time. Simple, child-like designs mingle with larger-than-life statues which could have been drawn by Modigliani and sculpted by Michaelangelo. The eagle warriors with their faces of aesthetes are fine examples of this.

Near the entrance on the ground floor is a model reconstruction of the ancient city. There are several of these in other museums but this one is by far the best. A glass model shows how the lakes in the Valley of Mexico have receded over the centuries.

The Templo Mayor Museum cannot be recommended too highly. It provides a magnificent review of a period in Mexican history that was obviously never meant to die. The monumental sculpture of Coyolxauhqui, whose discovery prompted a major excavation of the Aztec's Great Temple, can be seen on the second floor. She is represented in a decapitated and dismembered state just as is told in the legend of her fight with Huitzilopochtli. For over four hundred years this masterpiece had lain hidden at the base of the temple that the Spaniards had systematically destroyed. In 1978 she chose to rise again and show the world the glories that once were Tenochtitlán.

Museums in the University City Complex
Museos en la Ciudad Universitaria

Ciudad Universitaria

Insurgentes Sur s/n, Pedregal de San Angel

In the 1950s the whole of the National Autonomous University of Mexico was re-located to this enormous tract of land in the South of the city near Cuicuilco (see entry). The terrain was largely covered by lava rock from the eruption of the Xitle volcano. Then in 1968, the Olympic village was constructed in nearby Copilco for the games that were held in Mexico City that year. In fact, the whole area has been given a modernist treatment. The University City complex inspired the Jardines del Pedregal de San Angel which was in its day an ultra-modern residential section also built on the lava overflow from Xitle. In the late 1970s the Perisur shopping mall, which was the first of its kind in the country, was built almost opposite the ancient ceremonial site of Cuicuilco. More recently, a new cultural center has been opened in the midst of the university complex. The architectural styles are all extremely modern and the buildings comprise both research centers and places of entertainment. Of the latter, the Nezahualcóyatl concert hall is probably the best known and most frequented.

The university receives several thousands of visitors every year. Many of them come to admire two of the university's most famous landmarks: the administration building, with its murals by David Siqueiros, and the university library with its exterior murals by artist and architect, Juan O'Gorman. These library murals were done with tiny pieces of mosaic in natural colors and are very striking for this type of building.

It will come as no surprise to find that hidden away in this enormous complex are a motley group of museums. They are probably not of great interest to the general public although it is surprising how unpredictable that same public can be when to comes to deciding what arouses their sense of curiosity.

These university museums and collections are described below in their alphabetical order. The University City complex covers a vast area, so any more precise information regarding their location is best ascertained by asking the academic community on the campus.

The **Manuel H. Sarvide Museum of Anatomical Pathology** is to be found in the Faculty of Veterinary Medicine. The collection takes its name from a veterinary surgeon at the university who founded the museum in 1940. This impressive stockpile of animal remains is not to be visited by the faint-hearted. The diseased organs of even the most domesticated of animals are known to be unsettling, and they should always be kept strictly out of reach of children.

By contrast, the **University Museum of Anthropology** presents a far less violent spectacle. This collection inevitably pales in comparison with its national cousin in Chapultepec Park, but for the truly insatiable anthropologist it does provide yet another selection of masks and sundry archeological finds. It is housed in the Second Humanities Tower which impresses as being a wholly appropriate address.

A sortie into the **Faustino Miranda Botanical and Winter Garden** can be a relaxing alternative to viewing the seemingly limitless supply of potsherds. Mexican flora abounds here, and a stroll through these gardens can indeed be a most agreeable pastime. It appears however, that not only professional botanists are attracted to the bushes in the Faustino Miranda. For some, the pursuit of *flora mexicana* is most decidedly a lay pursuit. The gardens are run by the university's Institute of Botany and are entered on the football stadium side of Insurgentes Sur.

Returning indoors, but not leaving the botanical arena, one can enjoy the **Herbarium of the Faculty of Sciences**. If some plant specimens had remained undetected during one's romp through the Faustino Miranda, the herbarium will be sure to have them. This is a most complete collection of all known plant species in the Mexican Republic.

The **University Museum of Palaeontology** is distressingly similar to a load of old fossils. However, that is exactly as it should be, and if one were a professional palaeontologist or student of same, that would be good news. For the majority of us (i.e. those who have trouble spelling the word), we might be tempted to give the fossils a miss. However, if

129

the opportunity cannot be passed up, showcases full of the early imprints of human life on earth are to be found in the university's Institute of Geology.

The **University Museum of Sciences and Arts** is slightly more accessible to the non-academic visitor. This center, next to the Faculty of Architecture, mainly organizes temporary exhibitions.

The **Museum of Skeletons** needs no introduction. The danger of a an untoward meeting with one's great grandmother is no longer a possibility for the present day student of anatomy. Unlike his predecessor of a century ago, the modern student is now required to grapple with, and come to a lively understanding of, a skeleton model probably made in Stuttgart, West Germany. Not all the skeletons here are manufactured teaching aids. They still do preserve some human bones in the appropriate immersions. This collection is in the Department of Anatomy in the Faculty of Medicine.

Not far away in the Faculty of Veterinary Medicine is the **Veterinary Anatomy Museum**. In a nutshell, this collection provides more or less the same sort of stimulation as the skeleton museum does for the student of human anatomy.

Lastly, there is the **Alfonso L. Herrera Museum of Zoology** which is to be found in the Science Faculty. An uncountable number of native Mexican fauna specimens are on display here. This museum was opened in 1978, and its scope is impressive.

Museum of Watercolors
Museo de la Acuarela

Salvador Novo 88, Col. Sta. Catarina   Map 4

Open: Tuesday to Sunday 11.00 am to 6.00 pm

This pleasant, two-storey house in the middle of lush, sunny gardens belonging to the municipality of Coyoacán now houses a fine collection of Mexican watercolors from pre-Columbian times to the present.

The original museum, in the Colonia Roma, fell down in the 1985 earthquake and only sixty percent of the original collection was salvaged. The museum's director, Guati Rojo, himself a renowned Mexican watercolorist, has painstakingly devoted himself to restoring and renewing the collection. The upkeep is impeccable. The billowing *manta* (white cotton) curtains, polished wood floors, smooth freshly painted walls in pastel shades all combine to set the mood for watercolor.

Welcome to the house of paintings
All the colored waters
are the flowers I offer you.
(from a poem in room I)

Four and a half centuries ago, Mexicans painted in watercolor on bark or deerskin. These paintings, or codices, told the history of certain groups, explained religious beliefs or provided genealogical records and maps. Sadly, many of these originals are now to be found in European, rather than Mexican museums. The watercolor tradition was alive in Mexico long before the Spaniards arrived. In room one the museum's logo - the water flower and creative hand - is beautifully displayed in a block covered in *amatl* (a finely prepared surface of bark) and burnished with blue laquer. In pre-Columbian times, this flower was a symbol of the art of watercolor.

When codices were forbidden by the Spaniards, watercolor all but disappeared from Mexican art, not to reappear until the mid-nineteenth century. Many of the watercolorists who started painting then were a long-lived crowd, and some of the artists from the late 1980s were still painting in 1940. A good proportion of their work, ranging from the brilliant to the mediocre, is on display here. Few of the artists are known internationally, and probably the best known to Mexicans is the work of Saturnino Herrán.

The pretty gardens of the museum are often used for open air concerts, and the annex at the bottom of the garden is used for small, temporary exhibitions. Reproductions of the works displayed are on sale in the museum which also contains a small reference library for those interested in research on watercolor.

Mexico City Wax Museum
Museo de Cera de la Ciudad de México

Londres 6, Col. Juáraz   Map 5

Open: Monday to Sunday 11.00 am to 7.00 pm

Ever since Curtis and Marie Tussaud popularized wax repli-
cas over two hundred years ago, wax museums have been
popular with both children and adults. Perhaps the draw is
the macabre fascination of a technique that is closer to
embalming than sculpture. Mexico City's wax museum is a
delight, beginning with the doll's house perfection of the *art
nouveau* building which is its permanent home. The exterior
brick work is picked out in brown and and cream with dark-
green paint for the doors and iron work. Inside, natural light is
cleverly used to shine through the blues, yellows and or-
anges of the *art nouveau* stained-glass windows.

This is well worth a visit for its architectural value alone
(the mansion dates from 1901) and the sheer pleasure of
visiting any well-run museum. Adult visitors will enjoy getting
a glimpse of Mexican celebrities past and present (and several others of international renown). Children will have a ball
enjoying the chamber of horrors, which includes both Fran-
kenstein and Jack the Ripper at work, a torture chamber and
other ghoulish delights. However, the dramatic sacrifice of
the Aztec virgin is definitely the museum's *pièce de résistan-
ce*. If you do visit with young children, be prepared for them
to want to go round all over again. It is that compelling.

Adults will find the museum conveniently small. Wax
tends to be indigestible in large quantities. Nevertheless,
even after a visit here one still experiences the common phe-
nomenon of seeing how wax-like the first passers by seem
on leaving the building! Working in wax lends itself naturally
to humor, and the sleeping wax maintenance man in dirty
overalls placed in the museum's entrance is one such nice
touch.

So, who will you meet in the museum? Miguel Hidalgo,
Maximillian and Carlota are all here as is Benito Juárez with
his wife (she at work at her needlepoint, looking up with

The Mexican City Wax Museum

slightly veiled annoyance at having been interrupted). Both Emilio Zapata and Francisco Villa are represented as is Porfirio Díaz. Sor Juana Inés de la Cruz in her cell is another typical wax representative of Mexico's history in this museum. The Sor Juana model is a brilliant reconstruction of the famous Miguel Cabrera portrait in Chapultepec Castle. Only here, by contrast, she gazes contemplatively over the public lavatories! Fame brings no guarantee of respect.

At the more profane end of the historical spectrum, John Lennon, Muhammed Ali and Manolo Fábregas are all present along with an athletic, hairy-legged Hugo Sánchez who is taking a flying kick at a football.

Archeological Museum of Xochimilco
Museo Arqueológico de Xochimilco

Tenochtitlán 17, Pueblo de Santa Cruz, Xochimilco

Open: Tuesday to Sunday 10.00 am to 5.00 pm

The floating gardens of Xochimilco are one of the most popular tourist attractions that Mexico City has to offer. Particularly on Sundays and holidays, crowds arrive at the *embarcaderos* (landing stages) to hire one of the many brightly-painted, flat-bottomed boats known as *trajineras* for a boat trip around the canals of Xochimilco. Boatmen propel their boats with poles in ways similar to the gondolas of Venice or the punts of Oxford. Each boat has a canopy with a horseshoe arch at the forward end, the arch being decorated with flowers to form a woman's name such as *Rosita* or *Lupita*. Mariachi bands serenade couples from other barges while local women cook tacos and other Mexican specialities on small portable grills to sell to trippers as they pass by. A boat trip on the canals of Xochimilco is always a grand outing in full carnival style.

Xochimilco is a Nahuatl word meaning the place where flowers are cultivated. The Xochimilcas were one of the seven Nahua tribes who settled on the edges of the great lake around 900 A.D. The floating gardens, known as *chinampas*, were built on the shallow lake bed with earth brought from the surrounding hills. They were held together by aquatic vegetation layered into woven frames and anchored in the water with long stakes. Typical vegetation of the region included the *huejote* plant of the willow family which grows deep roots. Eventually, the roots of the *huejotes* anchored the *chinampas* permanently to the lake bed and a vast area of floating gardens interconnected by a labyrinthine system of canals was created. Each garden, being partially submerged in the water, became an extraordinarily fertile agricultural plot which yielded an abundance of fruit and vegetables. In Aztec times the produce was taken to market in Tenochtitlán by boat on the major La Viga canal which flowed into the city center. Xochimilco was also a major source of drinking water for Tenochtitlán with natural spring water from the surrounding hills being carried into the city by aqueducts.

With the drainage of large portions of the lake, Xochimilco shrank in size but it is still a very significant market area in Mexico City. Throughout the year a great variety of flowers, plants and vegetables are cultivated and in more modern times it has become an important manufacturing center for clothes, fabrics and ceramics. The present Xochimilco canal system still covers some two hundred kilometers of which only about four kilometers are used for tourist boat trips. Xochimilco is undoubtedly one of the few areas of Mexico City that has preserved much of its ancient pre-Hispanic culture and atmosphere.

The regional museum, housed in a European-style building from the early 1900s that used to be the waterworks, contains a rich collection of local fossils and archeological remains. There are two halls of permanent displays, one for temporary exhibitions and a center for the historical study of Xochimilco.

Unfortunately, the several showcases are not organized chronologically so one has to pay careful attention to the dates of each item displayed. Among the most interesting exhibits are the burial urns. For the Aztecs, cremation of the dead was a commonplace ritual which took the Spaniards by surprise. They considered such urns to be pots in which human flesh was cooked. Experts have long debated so-called Aztec cannibalism. Some contend that it never occured, others that it was a major source of protein and still others that it was a religious experience in a culture suffused with ritual. Some beautiful jade necklaces (this green stone was valued more than gold, and like feathers, it was reserved for priests and nobles only), children's toys and even a volcanic stone flat iron (the Aztecs ironed their clothes) are also exhibited. A collection of carved female figures are so detailed that one can clearly make out the hair styles and wraparound skirts that were then fashionable. Some of the carved animals - a life-size, pink-stoned jaguar and a rabbit in gray stone for example - are superb examples of pre-conquest sculpture. These rocks were sculpted with stone knives which must have required enormous patience and skill.

This is not an easy museum to find if one is new to Xochimilco. One is best advised to head for the canal area where the boats are hired and ask directions from there. By car, it takes about ten minutes from the landing stage and the museum is recognizable by the white wall which surrounds it in a square garden.

Alphabetical list of museums

Alameda Museum (Diego Rivera Mural) 15
Alfonso Reyes. House and Museum of 16
Anahuacalli Museum 18
Anthropology. National Museum of 21
Architecture. National Museum of 26
Art. National Museum of 26
Bellas Artes. Museum of the Palace of 29
Caricature. Museum of 31
Carranza. House and Museum of 32
Carrillo Gil Museum of Art 34
Cathedral Museum 36
Charrería. Museum of 39
Chopo University Museum 40
Contemporary Art Cultural Center 41
Cuicuilco Archeological Museum 42
Cultures. National Museum of 44
Diego Rivera Studio Museum 48
El Carmen. Museum of 51
Franz Mayer Museum 55
Frida Kahlo Museum 59
Geles Cabrera Museum of Sculpture 64
Geology Museum of the UNAM 65
Guadalupe Basilica Museum 65
History. National Museum of 68
History. Gallery of the National Museum
    of (Snail Museum) 72
Interventions. National Museum of 74
La Profesa. Art Gallery of the Church of 78
Leon Trotsky Museum 81
Marine Grotto 82
Mexican Clothing. Luis Márquez Romay Museum of 83
Mexican Medicine. Museum of the History of 84
Mexico City Museum 85
Modern Art. Museum of 89
Musical Instruments. National Museum of 91
National Palace. Museums in the 91
    Benito Juárez, Museum in Honor of
    Parliamentary Enclosure
Natural History Museum 94
Popular Arts and Industries. National Museum of 97

Popular Cultures. National Museum of   98
Postal Museum   99
Printing. National Museum of   100
Remembrance. Museum of   102
✗ Revolution. National Museum of the   103
Risco House Museum   107
Rufino Tamayo Museum   108
San Carlos Museum   109
San Diego. Viceroy Art Gallery of   111
Santo Domingo Cultural Center (Juan Cordero Room)   113
Siqueiros Public Art Gallery   114
Sor Juana Inés de la Cruz. Cloister of   115
Technology. Museum of   119
✗ Templo Mayor Museum   121
University City Complex. Museums in the   128
    Anatomical Pathology, Manuel H. Sarvide Museum of
    Anthropology. University Museum of
    Botanical and Winter Garden, The Faustino Miranda
    Herbarium of the Faculty of Sciences
    Palaeontology. University Museum of
    Sciences and Arts. University Museum of
    Skeletons. Museum of
    Veterinary Anatomy Museum
    Zoology. Alfonso L. Herrera Museum of
Watercolors. Museum of   130
Wax Museum. Mexico City   132
Xochimilco. Archeological Museum of   135

Museums of Mexico City
Map 1
(Historical Center)

1. San Carlos Museum
2. Alameda Museum (Diego Rivera mural)
3. Viceroy Art Gallery of San Diego
4. National Museum of Popular Arts and Industries
5. Franz Mayer Museum
6. National Museum of Printing
7. Museum of the Palace of Bellas Artes
8. Postal Museum
9. National Museum of Art
10. Cloister of Sor Juana Inés de la Cruz
    Luis Márquez Romay Museum
    of Mexican Clothing
11. Museum of Charrería
12. Art Gallery of the Church of La Profesa
13. Cathedral Museum
14. Mexico City Museum
15. Museum in Honor of Benito Juárez
16. Parliamentary Enclosure
17. Templo Mayor Museum
18. National Museum of Cultures

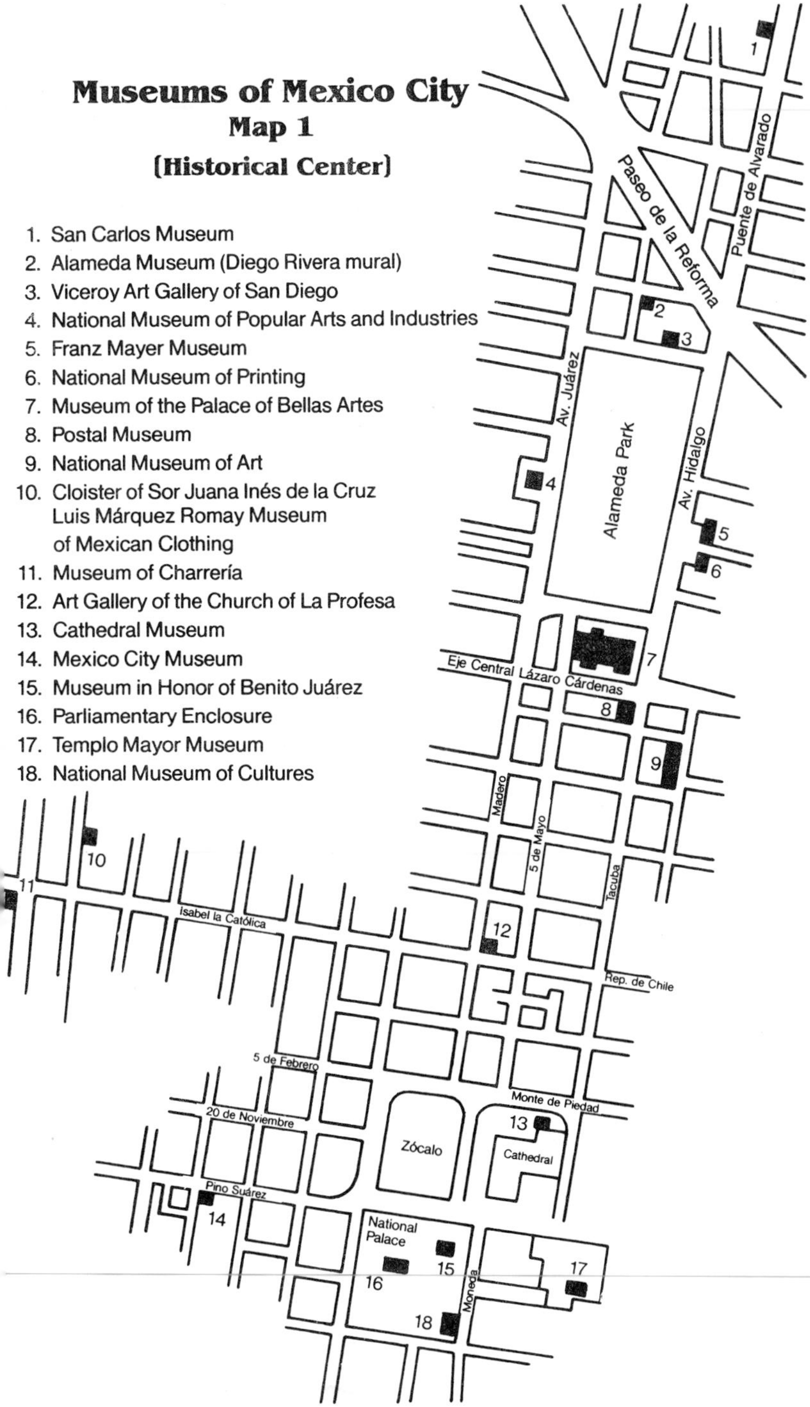

Paseo de la Reforma
Puente de Alvarado
Av. Juárez
Alameda Park
Av. Hidalgo
Eje Central Lázaro Cárdenas
Madero
5 de Mayo
Tacuba
Isabel la Católica
Rep. de Chile
5 de Febrero
20 de Noviembre
Monte de Piedad
Zócalo
Cathedral
Pino Suárez
National Palace
Moneda
1
2
3
4
5
6
7
8
9
10
11
12
13
14
15
16
17
18

Museums of Mexico City
Map 2
(San Angel Area)

1. San Angel Inn
2. Diego Rivera Studio Museum
3. Bazár Sábado
4. Risco House Museum
5. Carrillo Gil Museum of Art
6. Museum of El Carmen

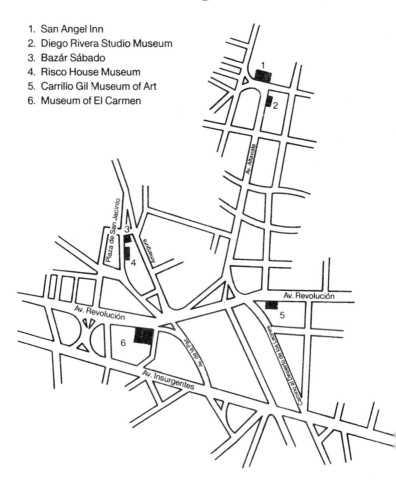

Museums of Mexico City
Map 3
[Chapultepec Park]

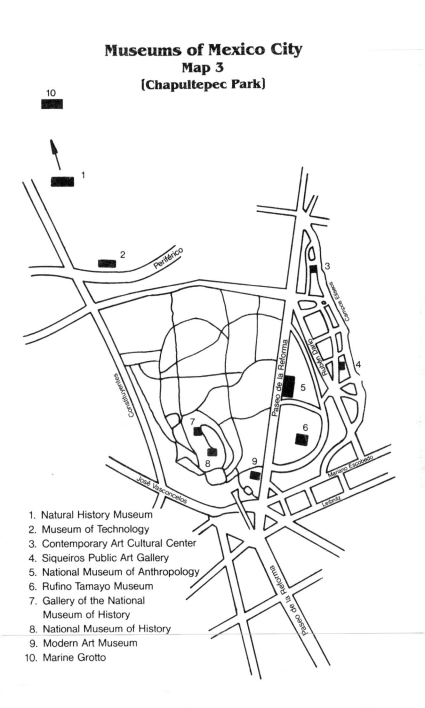

1. Natural History Museum
2. Museum of Technology
3. Contemporary Art Cultural Center
4. Siqueiros Public Art Gallery
5. National Museum of Anthropology
6. Rufino Tamayo Museum
7. Gallery of the National
   Museum of History
8. National Museum of History
9. Modern Art Museum
10. Marine Grotto

Museums of Mexico City
Map 4
[Coyoacán]

1. Museum of Watercolors
2. National Museum of Popular Cultures
3. Frida Kahlo Museum
4. Leon Trotsky Museum
5. National Museum of Interventions
6. Geles Cabrera Museum of Sculpture

Museums of Mexico City
Map 5
(Reforma-Insurgentes Area)

1. Geology Museum of the UNAM
2. Chopo University Museum
3. National Museum of the Revolution
4. Museum and House of Carranza
5. Mexico City Wax Museum
6. National Museum of Musical Instruments

Museums of Mexico City
Map 6

1. Santo Domingo Cultural Center
2. Museum of Mexican Medicine
3. Museum of Remembrance
4. Museum of Caricature

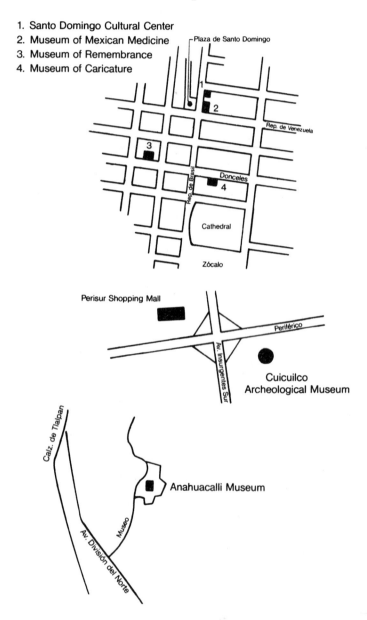

Head from Teotihuacán
The Anahuacalli Museum

Other Piramide Guides of interest

THE MEXICO CITY RESTAURANT GUIDE
Oriana Tickell de Castelló

An independent guide that accepts no advertising and no paid entries. Reviews seventy-five of the best restaurants in the city.

THE MEXICO CITY SHOPPING GUIDE
Candace Siegle

Reviews of over sixty of the best shops in Mexico City including markets and shops for arts and crafts, specialist silver shops and many other well-known stores offering ceramics, antiques, fabrics, miniatures, rugs and leather goods.

WALKING THROUGH HISTORY: A Series of Guided Walks through the Historic Center of Mexico City
Candace Siegle

Six guided walks covering all the major places of interest in Mexico's historic downtown area. Each walk is lavishly illustrated with some specially commissioned photographs by Keith Dannemiller. The text provides all the necessary historical and cultural background information to enable visitors to enjoy and appreciate their visit to this fascinating historic center to the full.

In preparation:

THE MEXICO CITY GUIDE
Michelle Da Silva Richmond

Este libro se terminó de imprimir
el día 31 de mayo de 1989.
La edición consta de 2,500 ejemplares.